AUSTRALIA VER ENGLAND
1861-2005
600 MEMORABLE MOMENTS

MARC DAWSON
Foreword by Jim Maxwell

ABC Books

Published by ABC Books for the
Australian Broadcasting Corporation
GPO Box 9994 Sydney NSW 2001

Copyright © Marc Dawson 2006

First published October 2006

All rights reserved. No part of this publication may be reproduced, stored in a retrieval system or transmitted in any form or by any means, electronic, mechanical, photocopying, recording or otherwise, without the prior written permission of the Australian Broadcasting Corporation

National Library of Australia
Cataloguing-in-Publication data

Dawson, Marc.
 Australia versus England 1861-2005: 600 memorable moments.

 ISBN 0 7333 1883 5

 1. Cricket -England -History. 2. Cricket - Australia - History. 3. Test matches (Cricket) - Australia - History. 4. Test matches (Cricket) - Australia - History. I. Australian Broadcasting Corporation. II. Title.

796.35865

Typeset in Galliard 9/11pt and designed in InDesign by Anna Warren, Warren Ventures
Cover design by Anna Warren
Project management by Richard Smart Publishing
Printed in Australia by McPherson's Printing Group

54321

Contents

Foreword by Jim Maxwell	5
1861-1899	7
1901-1912	43
1919-1938	57
1945-1968	81
1970-2005	101
Australia Versus England Test Match Results 1877-2005	166

ACKNOWLEDGMENTS

REFERENCES

Books

Philip Bailey, Philip Thorn and Peter Wynne-Thomas, *Who's Who of Cricketers*, Guild Publishing, London, 1984

Bill Frindall, *The Wisden Book of Test Cricket*, Macdonald & Co Ltd, London, 1985

David Frith, *England v Australia Test Match Records*, Willow Books, London, 1986

Allan Miller, *Allan's Australian Cricket Annual*, Allan Miller, Busselton, various years

Charlie Watt, *Australian First-class Cricket*, Five Mile Press, Knoxfield, 1993

Ray Webster and Allan Miller, *First-Class Cricket in Australia: 1850-51 to 1941-42*, Ray Webster, Glen Waverley, 1993

Wisden Cricketers' Almanack, John Wisden & Co Ltd, Guildford, various years

Peter Wynne-Thomas, *The Complete History of Cricket Tours*, Hamlyn, London, 1989

Newspapers
The Age, The Australian, The Canberra Times, The Daily Telegraph, Herald Sun, The Sun-Herald, Sunday Telegraph, Sydney Morning Herald

Websites
www.abc.net.au/cricket; www.bbc.co.uk/tms; www.channel4.com/sport/cricket; www.cricket.com.au; www.cricinfo.com; www.cricket-archive.co.uk; www.howstat.com.au/cricket; www.thatscricket.com

Illustration on page 101
First-day cover, 2005, reproduced by permission of Norvic Philatelics, Norfolk, England; the urn by permission of the Marylebone Cricket Club; the three-lions logo by permission of the England and Wales Cricket Board.

FOREWORD

For sports trivia buffs cricket is a statistical lifeline, and Marc Dawson's latest collection provides yet another plentiful source for fans of this fascinating and unique game.

Marc's memorable moment number 192 mentions Roy Park's first-ball duck at the MCG in the 1920-21 Ashes series. There's a nice embellishment to his story. It was Dr Park's only Test innings, and his mother allegedly missed his entire Test batting career because she dropped her knitting and looked away for the millisecond it took Harry Howell to bowl him. Memorable moment 359 covers Graham Gooch's pair on debut in 1975: the self-effacing player later described this as the only instance of a Test cricketer having his maiden, and perhaps any, pair of Test innings contained in his name.

Marc has thoughtfully included memorable moments not only from the Ashes series but also the whole of Australia versus England cricket history. Here's an interesting entrepreneurial postscript to add to memorable moment number 1 that covers the first visit to Australia by English cricketers, in 1861-62. The English publicans Felix Spiers and Christopher Pond who underwrote the tour, paying £2000 plus all expenses to 13 players, profited handsomely, earning over £11,000. And their windfall was matched by Dr W.G. Grace, the legendary amateur champion of the Victorian era, who was later enticed to return to Australia by Lord Sheffield in 1891-92 at the age of 43. He was paid £3000, plus expenses, and provided with a locum for his medical practice in Gloucestershire. Sheffield, who sponsored Grace's 'amateur' tour, didn't fare as well losing £2000. His legacy, however, was the Sheffield Shield, the interstate trophy that existed until other commercial interests took over. The Shield was awarded for the last time in 1998-99.

The first-ever cricket tour of England in 1868 was by a team of Aborigines (memorable moment 8), and it was also the first-ever tour by any Australian sporting team. Johnny Mullagh's all-round feats must have been wearying: the team only had fourteen rest days in five months as they zig-zagged England. They played 47 matches and complemented their cricketing prowess with traditional skills such as boomerang throwing.

An interesting highlight of the Third Test at the Adelaide Oval in 1924-25 was that it marked radio's Test debut, with Bill Smallacombe providing descriptions on the new-fangled wireless. Local radio dealers erected receivers in their doorways, and avid fans stood listening to the broadcast for hours. Smallacombe, who called every ball of the match, found it strained his vocal chords, and in an attempt to find something interesting to say when play was slow he offered comments about ladies' fashions.

Marc refers to the birth of the Ashes in 1882 (memorable moment 35), when Fred Spofforth bowled Australia to a shock seven-run victory at The Oval. Reginald Brooks' mock obituary in *The Sporting Times* newspaper, stating that 'the body will be cremated and the ashes taken to Australia', was a piece of satire, because at the time cremation was illegal. England's captain, the Hon. Ivo Bligh, was presented with the ashes of a burnt bail during the 1882-83 tour, but when Australia levelled the series two-all Bligh said that the revered Ashes should be buried at the MCG as his team was going home without them.

If Australia regain the Ashes in the 2006–07 summer, imagine the clamour for the famous urn to be repossessed, or even highjacked, on its ceremonial tour here. Like one of the original convicts, the urn's being temporarily transported to the colonies.

Jim Maxwell

Jim Maxwell has been one of ABC Radio cricket's most highly recognised and regarded broadcasters for thirty years. He's been covering Test matches the world over since 1977, and during the 2006–07 Ashes series will post his double-century of Test calls.

1861–1899

THE ALL ENGLAND ELEVEN.—ARRIVAL AT THE CAFE DE PARIS, MELBOURNE.

AUSTRALIA VERSUS ENGLAND 1861-2005

1861-62
TOUR OF AUSTRALIA

1 The first cricket tour of Australia took place in 1861-62 when a team of English players accepted an invitation from the Melbourne catering firm Spiers and Pond. The first 'international match' in Australia began on New Year's Day in 1862 and resulted in an innings victory for the Englishmen (305) over the Eighteen of Victoria (118 & 91) in Melbourne. Three of the English bowlers claimed seven wickets in an innings – George Griffith (7-30), George Bennett (7-53) and Tom Sewell (7-20), while two scored half-centuries – William Caffyn (79) and Griffith (61). At the end of the match, a giant balloon – featuring portraits of the England cricketers – was launched from the MCG to celebrate the historic event.

2 Yorkshire's Roger Iddison took 19 wickets (8-32 & 11-63) against a Tasmanian Twenty-Two at Hobart. In his next appearance – an 11-a-side exhibition match – he claimed 7 for 52 and finished the tour on a high note with 22 wickets (9-37 & 13-168) against a Victorian XXII in Melbourne.

3 In a three-day match billed as 'Surrey v The World' at the MCG – the two teams a mixture of the English tourists and Victorians – Kent's George Bennett turned in an exceptional all-round double, scoring 72 in his only innings and taking 7 for 30 and 7 for 85.

THE TOURISTS

H.H. Stephenson (c), G. Bennett, W. Caffyn, G. Griffith,
T. Hearne, R. Iddison, C. Lawrence, W. Mortlock, W. Mudie,
T. Sewell, E. Stephenson, C. Wells.

THE RESULTS

FIRST-CLASS MATCHES				ALL MATCHES			
P	W	L	D	P	W	L	D
–	–	–	–	12	6	2	4

1863-64
TOUR OF AUSTRALIA

4 In a match against an Ararat Twenty-Two, England's bowlers dismissed 25 batsmen for a duck, with six making pairs. In the local team's first innings scoreline of 35, the first nine batsmen failed to score.

5 Nottinghamshire's Bob 'Spider' Tinley, one of the leading exponents of 'lob' bowling, took an extraordinary 117 wickets in his first five matches – 19 for 115 against a Victorian XXII at Melbourne, 27 for 57 v Bendigo XXII, 23 for 70 v Ballarat XXII, 26 for 45 v Ararat XXII and 22 for 72 against a Maryborough XXII. He finished the tour with 171 wickets, average 3.65.

6 Victoria's Tom Wills took three wickets in four balls for G. Anderson's XI against G. Parr's XI at Melbourne, becoming the first bowler to achieve the feat in a first-class match against an English team.

7 In the penultimate match of the tour, against a Ballarat Twenty-Two, Cambridgeshire's Bob Carpenter, with 121, scored the first century by an English tourist in Australia.

THE TOURISTS

G. Parr (c), G. Anderson, J. Caesar, W. Caffyn, R. Carpenter, A. Clarke, E.M. Grace, T. Hayward, J. Jackson, T. Lockyer, G. Tarrant, R.C. Tinley.

THE RESULTS

FIRST-CLASS MATCHES				ALL MATCHES			
P	W	L	D	P	W	L	D
–	–	–	–	16	10	0	6

ptember
1868
TOUR OF ENGLAND

8 The first-ever cricket tour of England was undertaken by a team of Australian Aborigines in 1868. The trip was financed by G.W. Graham and George Smith, with the team captained by Charles Lawrence, a Surrey cricketer who had stayed behind in Australia after touring with the England side in 1861-62. A gruelling program of 47 matches was played, the Aborigines winning 14 and losing 14. The first match was against the Surrey Club at The Oval, in which Lawrence took 7 for 91. Johnny Mullagh, who scored 73 in the Surrey match, finished the tour with 1698 runs and 257 wickets, while Cuzens scored 1358 runs and took 114 wickets.

THE TOURISTS

C. Lawrence (c), Bullocky, Charley, Cuzens, Dick-a-Dick, Jim Crow, King Cole, Mosquito, J. Mullagh, Peter, Red Cap, Sundown, Tiger, Twopenny.

THE RESULTS

FIRST-CLASS MATCHES				ALL MATCHES			
P	W	L	D	P	W	L	D
-	-	-	-	47	14	14	19

1873-74
TOUR OF AUSTRALIA

9 The great W.G. Grace made his first tour of Australia in 1873-74, beginning the campaign with a double of 10 wickets in an innings and 51* against Eighteen of Victoria at Melbourne. In the next match, at Bendigo, W.G. scored 126, while his brother, G.F., made 112 in England's only innings of 470.

10 Martin McIntyre, from Nottinghamshire, almost single-handedly destroyed the Yorke's Peninsula XXII team (42 & 13) at Kadina in South Australia, returning the remarkable figures of 9 for 4 and 7 for 1. The local team's second-innings effort of 13 is the lowest-ever total against an English team in Australia, and it included 12 ducks and just eight runs off the bat.

THE TOURISTS

W.G. Grace (c), F.H. Boult, J.A. Bush, W.R. Gilbert,
G.F. Grace, A. Greenwood, T. Humphrey, H. Jupp,
J. Lillywhite, M. McIntyre, W. Oscroft, J. Southerton.

THE RESULTS

FIRST-CLASS MATCHES				ALL MATCHES			
P	W	L	D	P	W	L	D
–	–	–	–	15	10	3	2

1876-77
TOUR OF AUSTRALIA

11 England undertook its first fully professional tour of Australia in 1876-77. Sussex cricketer James Lillywhite arranged, captained and managed the side. Fifteen matches were played, three of which had first-class status.

12 The first first-class match between an England team and an Australian team began on 15 January 1877 at the Albert Ground in Sydney. Alec Bannerman and Tom Garrett, who would both later play Test cricket, made their first-class debuts for New South Wales. George Ulyett top-scored in the match for J. Lillywhite's England XI, with 94. Edwin Evans took 5 for 96 for NSW, while Alfred Shaw was the best with the ball, taking 5 for 19 and 4 for 35.

AUSTRALIA VERSUS ENGLAND 1861-2005

13 A hastily-arranged match between the England side and a combined New South Wales-Victoria XI at the MCG in March is later recognised as the inaugural Test match. The Australians (245 & 104), captained by Dave Gregory, beat England (196 & 108) by 45 runs in front of a total crowd estimated at 20,500. Charles Bannerman, who batted in the middle-order for New South Wales, went in first with Nat Thomson, and scored the first run and the first Test century – his only hundred in first-class cricket. His undefeated innings of 165 – he retired hurt – represented 67.34 per cent of Australia's total of 245, an Ashes record. Yorkshire's Allen Hill clean-bowled Thomson for one, capturing the first Test wicket, while Australia's Billy Midwinter claimed Test cricket's first five-wicket haul (5-78). Ned Gregory scored the first Test duck. Tom Garrett made his Test debut aged 18, and remained Australia's youngest Test cricketer for some 75 years.

14 On his Test debut, in the second match at Melbourne, Victorian batsman Thomas Kelly struck eight successive hits for four during his second-innings knock of 35.

THE TOURISTS

J. Lillywhite (c), T. Armitage, H.R.J. Charlwood,
T. Emmett, A. Greenwood, A. Hill, H. Jupp, E. Pooley,
J. Selby, A. Shaw, J. Southerton, G. Ulyett.

THE RESULTS

TEST MATCHES	FIRST-CLASS MATCHES	ALL MATCHES
P W L D	P W L D	P W L D
2 1 1 0	3 1 1 1	15 5 4 6

1st Test Melbourne: Australia won by 45 runs
2nd Test Melbourne: England won by 4 wickets

1878
TOUR OF ENGLAND

15 The 1878 tourists were dismissed for under 100 in each innings (63 & 76) by Nottinghamshire in Australia's first first-class match in England. Alfred Shaw was the Notts' match-winner, taking 5 for 20 and 6 for 35. Billy Midwinter became the first Australian batsman in first-class cricket to carry his bat, with 16* in the their second-innings total of 76.

16 The bowling of Fred Spofforth dominated the second match of the tour, against the MCC (33 & 19) at Lord's, with the New South Wales speedster taking 6 for 4 and 4 for 16. Victoria's 'Harry' Boyle, in his first match in England, took 6 for 3 in the MCC's innings of 19. The entire match lasted just six hours, with only 105 runs scored – the lowest completed-match aggregate on record in first-class cricket. The Australians made 41 and 1-12, gaining victory by a margin of nine wickets.

17 One of the most bizarre episodes in the history of the game took place during the match with Middlesex at Lord's, when W.G. Grace 'kidnapped' Australian batsman Billy Midwinter. Padded up and about to open the Australian innings with Charles Bannerman, Grace convinced Midwinter to play for his native Gloucestershire in a match against Surrey across town at The Oval. Midwinter complied and did not play for the Australians again on tour.

18 Charles Bannerman, who scored the first-ever Test century, also scored the first century by an Australian tourist in England, with 133* against Leicestershire, although the match was not first-class. Fred Spofforth, who took the most first-class wickets (97 at 11.00) on tour, had the distinction of scoring the first first-class fifty – 56 v Middlesex at Lord's. The highest first-class tour score came from Charles Bannerman's brother, Alec, who carried his bat for 71* against Orleans Club at Twickenham.

19 In a first-class match against the Players at The Oval, Surrey's slow left-arm bowler Ted Barratt took all 10 wickets in an innings for 43 runs, with Australia dismissed for just 77. This is the lowest completed total in a first-class match involving an Australian team to include a half-century (Charles Bannerman 51). Despite Barratt's outstanding performance, the Australians won the match, thanks to Fred Spofforth, who took 7 for 37 and 5 for 38. He also claimed a hat-trick, his second in first-class matches on the tour.

THE TOURISTS

D.W. Gregory (c), F.E. Allan, G.H.T. Bailey,
A.C. Bannerman, C. Bannerman, J.McC. Blackham,
H.F. Boyle, J. Conway, T.W. Garrett, T.P. Horan,
W.E. Midwinter, W.L. Murdoch, F.R Spofforth.
(Reinforcement: H.W. Tennant).

THE RESULTS

TEST MATCHES	FIRST-CLASS MATCHES	ALL MATCHES
P W L D	P W L D	P W L D
– – – –	15 7 4 4	37 18 7 12

1878-79
TOUR OF AUSTRALIA

20 In the Test match at Melbourne, the only one played in 1878-79, Fred Spofforth dismissed Vernon Royle, Francis MacKinnon and Tom Emmett with successive balls to secure the first Test hat-trick. He went on to become the first bowler to take 10 wickets in a Test, with 13 for 110. Australia's opening batsmen both made the same scores in each innings – Charles Bannerman (15 & 15*) and Billy Murdoch (4 & 4*). England's wicket-keeper Leland Hone made his only Test appearance and was the first cricketer to play for England who had never represented a first-class county.

21 The second match between Lord Harris' England XI and New South Wales made headlines with a pitch invasion on the second day. After becoming the first batsman to carry his bat in a first-class match in Australia (82*), Billy Murdoch was adjudged run out for 10 in the second innings by umpire George Coulthard. Upset at the ruling, Dave Gregory refused to send in the next batsman and when the English players moved towards the pavilion, a section of the crowd stormed the field and set upon a number of the players. The other umpire in this match was Edmund Barton, who would later become Australia's first Prime Minister. England's

George Ulyett, with 4 for 13 in the second innings, became the first bowler to take four wickets in four balls in a first-class match in Australia.

22 In the game against an England XI at the MCG, Victoria's wicket-keeper Jack Blackham achieved the first instance of five stumpings in an innings in a first-class match in Australia.

23 The first Aborigine to play first-class cricket for Victoria, Johnny Mullagh, made his debut in England's final tour match of the season at the MCG. He top-scored for Victoria in the second innings with 36.

THE TOURISTS

Lord Harris (c), C.A. Absolom, T. Emmett, L. Hone,
A.N. Hornby, A.P. Lucas, H.C. Maul, F.A. MacKinnon,
F. Penn, V.P.F.A. Royle, S.S. Schultz, A.J. Webbe.

THE RESULTS

TEST MATCHES	FIRST-CLASS MATCHES	ALL MATCHES
P W L D	P W L D	P W L D
1 0 1 0	5 2 3 0	13 5 3 5

Only Test Melbourne: Australia won by 10 wickets

1880
TOUR OF ENGLAND

24 Fifteen players made their debuts in the Test match at The Oval. Of the eight newcomers for England, three came from the Grace family of Gloucestershire, brothers W.G., E.M. and G.F. – the first instance of three brothers playing in the same Test. Opening the batting with E.M. in the first innings, W.G. scored 152, England's first Test century. G.F., who made a duck batting at No.9 in the first innings, opened the second innings with similar misfortune and recorded the first pair in Test cricket. Captaining Australia for the first time, Billy Murdoch experienced mixed fortunes with the bat, scoring both a duck and a century. His 153* was the first century by a Test captain and the first first-class century by an Australian tourist in England.

25 In the final match of the tour, against the Players at Crystal Palace, 'Harry' Boyle (7-80) and George Palmer (11-89) became the first Australians to bowl unchanged throughout both completed innings of a first-class match in England.

26 Although hampered by injury throughout the tour, Fred Spofforth topped the first-class tour averages with 40 wickets at 8.40. He took five wickets in an innings six times, with a best return of 8 for 61 against Derbyshire. In all matches Spofforth took a phenomenal 391 wickets at 5.63.

THE TOURISTS

W.L. Murdoch (c), G. Alexander, A.C. Bannerman,
J.McC. Blackham, G.J. Bonnor, H.F. Boyle, T.U. Groube,
A.H. Jarvis, P.S. McDonnell, W.H. Moule, G.E. Palmer,
J. Slight, F.R. Spofforth.
(Reinforcements: W.A. Giles, A. McDonald).

THE RESULTS

TEST MATCHES	FIRST-CLASS MATCHES	ALL MATCHES
P W L D	P W L D	P W L D
1 0 1 0	9 4 2 3	37 21 4 12

Only Test The Oval: England won by 5 wickets

1881-82
Tour of Australia

27 An up-and-coming bowler from country-New South Wales burst onto the scene in 1881-82 in a match for the Bathurst Twenty-Two against Alfred Shaw's England team. After the visitors had lost their first three batsmen in the first innings, Charlie Turner came on and took the remaining 17 wickets (7-33 & 10-36).

28 In the match against New South Wales at Sydney, England captain Alfred Shaw recorded one of first-class cricket's most inexpensive analyses, and the finest in Australia. In the second innings he allowed just four scoring strokes, returning the miserly figures of 29-25-5-3.

29 In a match played out to the finish at the MCG in December, an England XI (146 & 198) defeated Victoria (251 & 75) by 18 runs, becoming the first team in Australian first-class cricket to follow-on and gain victory.

30 Billy Midwinter, who played for Australia in the first two Test matches in 1876-77, made his debut for England in the first Test at Melbourne. James Lillywhite, who captained England in 1876-77, became the first former Test cricketer to umpire a Test match. Tom Horan (124) and George Giffen (30) shared Australia's first century partnership – 107 for the fifth wicket. This was the first first-class match in Australia, and the first Test, to produce 1000 runs (England 294 & 308, Australia 320 & 3-127).

31 In the second match at Sydney, Australia's George Palmer (7-68) and Edwin Evans (3-64) became the first pair to bowl unchanged in a completed Test innings, dismissing England for 133. George Ulyett (67) and Dick Barlow (62) opened the second innings with 122 – the first hundred opening partnership in Tests. George Coulthard became the first Test umpire to play in a Test match. A 'one-Test wonder', Coulthard scored 6* in his only innings and returned to umpiring duties in the fourth Test at Melbourne.

32 Opening the batting in the fourth Test, George Ulyett (149) scored England's first first-class century in Australia. Billy Murdoch (85) and Alec Bannerman (37) recorded Australia's first century opening partnership with 110. This was the last drawn Test match in Australia until 1946-47.

THE TOURISTS

A. Shaw (c), R.G. Barlow, W. Bates, T. Emmett, J. Lillywhite, W.E. Midwinter, E. Peate, R. Pilling, W.H. Scotton, J. Selby, A. Shrewsbury, G. Ulyett.

THE RESULTS

TEST MATCHES	FIRST-CLASS MATCHES	ALL MATCHES
P W L D	P W L D	P W L D
4 0 2 2	7 3 2 2	18 8 3 7

1st Test Melbourne: Drawn
2nd Test Sydney: Australia won by 5 wickets
3rd Test Sydney: Australia won by 6 wickets
4th Test Melbourne: Drawn

1882
TOUR OF ENGLAND

33 New South Wales batsman Hugh Massie christened the opening tour match, against Oxford University, with a maiden first-class century (206) – the first first-class double-century by an Australian tourist in England. He reached 100* in the opening session of play, becoming the first Australian batsman to score a century before lunch on the first day of a first-class match. This was the only century of his first-class career.

34 In the first-class match at Cambridge, University all-rounder Charles Studd took 5 for 64 and scored 118, becoming the first player to achieve the double of five wickets in an innings and a century in the same match against an Australian team.

35 Of the 33 first-class matches on tour, the only Test played gave birth to The Ashes. Gaining victory by seven runs at The Oval, Australia's first Test win in England was 'commemorated' by the *Sporting Times* with a mock obituary, stating that the body of English cricket would be cremated and the ashes sent to Australia. Fred Spofforth was the match-winner with seven wickets in each innings – the first bowler to take 14 wickets in a Test. In his first-innings haul of 7 for 46, he bowled 10 maidens in his last 11 overs, and recorded Test cricket's first instance of three wickets in four balls. This was the first Test match to be completed in two days.

36 J.T. Parnham (5-101 & 7-25) took 12 wickets on his debut in first-class cricket, for a United England XI against the Australians at Tunbridge Wells.

THE TOURISTS

W.L. Murdoch (c), A.C. Bannerman, J.McC. Blackham,
G.J. Bonnor, H.F. Boyle, T.W. Garrett, G. Giffen,
T.P. Horan, S.P. Jones, P.S. McDonnell, H.H. Massie,
G.E. Palmer, F.R. Spofforth.
(Reinforcement: C.W. Beal).

THE RESULTS

TEST MATCHES	FIRST-CLASS MATCHES	ALL MATCHES
P W L D	P W L D	P W L D
1 0 1 0	33 18 4 11	38 23 4 11

Only Test The Oval: Australia won by 7 runs

1882-83
TOUR OF AUSTRALIA

37 Prior to a match against Ballarat, the English cricketers, led by the Hon. Ivo Bligh, were guests at Rupertswood, the Sunbury residence of the Melbourne Cricket Club President Sir William Clarke and his wife Lady Clarke. On Christmas Eve, a social game of cricket was played on the lawns of the mansion and it was here that one of sports' greatest trophies came into existence. After the appearance of the *Sporting Times* obituary notice three months previously, and the captain's pledge to retrieve 'The Ashes' of English cricket, Lady Clarke presented Bligh with a souvenir to commemorate the match at Rupertswood. It was the ashes of a burnt bail, or a ball, placed in a small urn, a trophy that resides in the MCC Museum at Lord's.

38 The first three Tests of 1882-83 were originally billed as 'Mr Murdoch's Eleven v The Hon. Ivo Bligh's Team'. Ivo Bligh captained England on his Test debut, in the first Test at the MCG, and marked his appearance with a first-innings duck. Bligh led England in the following three Tests as well, these four matches representing his entire Test career.

39 Billy Bates turned in a history-making performance in the second Test at Melbourne, capturing England's first Test hat-trick (Percy McDonnell, George Giffen, George Bonnor). His three-in-three formed part of an eventual match-haul of 14 wickets and with a knock of 55 in England's only innings, he became the first player to take 10 wickets and score a half-century in the same Test. England won the match within three days, recording the first victory by an innings margin in Test cricket.

40 The third Test, in Sydney, which was won by England, saw Edmund Tylecote (66) become the first wicket-keeper to score a 50 in Test cricket. Having successfully fulfilled his pledge to bring back the 'Ashes', Ivo Bligh and his side competed in a fourth Test match, again at the SCG. It was in this game that Jack Blackham scored 57 and 58* – the first wicket-keeper to score two half-centuries in a Test match. Billy Midwinter played for Australia again, after appearing four times for England. George Bonnor was reported to have been put down at least eight times during his knock of 87 (the first Australian batsman to be dismissed for what is regarded as the country's unluckiest score). As many as five of the dropped catches were attributed to Allan Steel, the man who eventually went on to take his wicket. In the second innings, Billy Murdoch batted for 70 minutes before getting off the mark.

THE TOURISTS

Hon. I.F.W. Bligh (c), R.G. Barlow, W. Barnes, W. Bates,
C.F.H. Leslie, F. Morley, W.W. Read, A.G. Steel, C.T. Studd,
G.B. Studd, E.F.S. Tylecote, G.F. Vernon.

THE RESULTS

TEST MATCHES	FIRST-CLASS MATCHES	ALL MATCHES
P W L D	P W L D	P W L D
4 2 2 0	7 4 3 0	17 9 3 5

1st Test Melbourne: Australia won by 9 wickets
2nd Test Melbourne: England won by an innings and 27 runs
3rd Test Sydney: England won by 69 runs
4th Test Sydney: Australia won by 4 wickets

1884
TOUR OF ENGLAND

41 In the second innings of the match against an England XI in Birmingham, Fred Spofforth recorded the remarkable first-class figures of 7 for 3 off 8.3 overs, after taking 7 for 34 in the first. The Australians (76 & 6-33) defeated the England XI (82 & 26) on the first day.

42 Australia's George Giffen became the first player in first-class cricket to score a century and take a hat-trick in the same match, performing the feat against Lancashire at Manchester. With 113 and 6 for 55 he was also the first Australian to score a century and take five wickets in an innings in the same first-class match.

43 In the first-ever Test match played at Lord's, Australia's captain Billy Murdoch caught his team-mate 'Tup' Scott in the first innings, becoming the first substitute to take a catch in Test cricket.

44 In the third Test, at The Oval, Billy Murdoch scored 211, the first double-century in Test-match cricket. Percy McDonnell (103) and 'Tup' Scott (102) also made centuries, in a total of 551 – the first time 500 had been scored in a Test innings. For England, Walter Read chipped in with 117 off 36 scoring strokes, the highest innings in Test cricket by a No.10 batsman. For the first time in Test history, all eleven players bowled, in Australia's first innings. The most successful with the ball was the wicket-keeper, Alfred Lyttelton, who, bowling underarm, took 4 for 19 off 12 overs. W.G. Grace kept wicket to Lyttelton, and took a catch off the first delivery he received behind the stumps at Test level.

45 Dick Barlow scored 101 and took 4 for 6 and 6 for 42 for North of England against the Australians at Nottingham. His all-round double was the first instance of 100 runs and 10 wickets in a match by an English player against Australia.

46 Fred Spofforth amassed 205 first-class scalps on tour, the first Australian bowler to exceed 200 wickets in an English season.

THE TOURISTS

W.M. Murdoch (c), G. Alexander, A.C. Bannerman, J.McC. Blackham, G.J. Bonnor, H.F. Boyle, W.H. Cooper, G. Giffen, P.S. McDonnell, W.E. Midwinter, G.E. Palmer, H.J.H. Scott, F.R. Spofforth. (Reinforcement: C. Lord).

THE RESULTS

TEST MATCHES	FIRST-CLASS MATCHES	ALL MATCHES
P W L D	P W L D	P W L D
3 0 1 2	31 17 7 7	32 18 7 7

1st Test Manchester: Drawn
2nd Test Lord's: England won by an innings and 5 runs
3rd Test The Oval: Drawn

1884-85
TOUR OF AUSTRALIA

47 Adelaide's first Test match saw Percy McDonnell (124) become the first batsman to score two hundreds in successive Test innings, having made 103 at The Oval in 1884.

48 Nine Australians made their Test debuts in the second match, at Melbourne, after the first-Test eleven was not considered for selection after demanding an increase in payment. Five of the new faces – Alfred Marr, Sam Morris, Harry Musgrove, Roland Pope and 'Digger' Robertson – were never chosen again. For the first time, players from the same county occupied England's first three spots in the batting order – Nottinghamshire's Arthur Shrewsbury, William Scotton and Billy Barnes.

49 Against the Twenty-Two of Moss Vale in New South Wales, Bobby Peel took 18 wickets for 7 runs with the home-side demolished for just 14! His wickets came at an average of just 0.38 runs per batsman.

50 In the third Test at Sydney, Australia gained victory by just six runs. Fred Spofforth collected 10 wickets in the match, including England's first three first-innings wickets in four balls. Billy Barnes, who topped England's first-class bowling averages on the tour, refused to bowl in the second innings in protest at not being allowed to bowl in the first.

51 In the fourth match at Sydney, George Bonnor (128) reached 100, for the only time in his Test career, in 100 minutes – at the time, the fastest hundred in Test cricket.

52 Arthur Shrewsbury made 105* in the fifth Test at Melbourne, becoming the first England captain to score a Test century. Fred Spofforth (50) top-scored in the first innings, becoming the first Australian No.11 to score a half-century. E.H. Elliot, appointed as one of the umpires, died a few days before the Test began and was replaced by G.J. Hodges. Following complaints about his performance by the England team, Hodges withdrew on the third day, resulting in Tom Garrett, a player in the match, being called on to deputise. Patrick McShane made his Test debut for Australia, having umpired the previous Test.

53 For the first time in Test cricket, one country, Australia, used as many as four captains in a single series. Billy Murdoch captained the first Test, Tom Horan the second and fifth, Hugh Massie the third and Jack Blackham the fourth.

THE TOURISTS

A. Shrewsbury (c), W. Attewell, W. Barnes, W. Bates,
J. Briggs, W. Flowers, J. Hunter, J. Lillywhite, R. Peel,
J.M. Read, W.H. Scotton, A. Shaw, G. Ulyett.

AUSTRALIA VERSUS ENGLAND 1861-2005

THE RESULTS

TEST MATCHES	FIRST-CLASS MATCHES	ALL MATCHES
P W L D	P W L D	P W L D
5 3 2 0	8 6 2 0	33 16 2 15

1st Test Adelaide: England won by 8 wickets
2nd Test Melbourne: England won by 10 wickets
3rd Test Sydney: Australia won by 6 runs
4th Test Sydney: Australia won by 8 wickets
5th Test Melbourne: England won by an innings and 98 runs

1886
TOUR OF ENGLAND

54 In the tour match against Oxford University, Fred Spofforth took his third career-haul of nine wickets in a first-class innings. His 9 for 18, off 13 overs, remains one of the game's best returns.

55 During his knock of 67* against Yorkshire at Sheffield, 'Tup' Scott hit 22 (6, 4, 6, 6) runs from one over sent down by Saul Wade, the world record for a four-ball over in first-class cricket.

56 In the second Test at Lord's, Arthur Shrewsbury made 164, to record the highest individual score to date by an England Test cricketer. W.G. Grace regained the record in the following Test at The Oval, with 170. Australia lost all three Test matches, the final two by an innings margin.

57 George Giffen, who topped the first-class batting averages (1424 runs at 26.86), took the most wickets on tour, with 154, average 17.36, becoming the first Australian to secure the double in an English season. He claimed five wickets in an innings on 13 occasions, and during the course of five first-class innings took a record 40 wickets – 7-41 & 9-60 v Derbyshire at Derby, 8-56 v Cambridge University at Cambridge and 8-23 & 8-42 v Lancashire at Old Trafford.

THE TOURISTS

H.J.H. Scott (c), J.McC. Blackham, G.J. Bonnor, W. Bruce,
E. Evans, T.W. Garrett, G. Giffen, A.H. Jarvis, S.P. Jones,
J. McIlwraith, G.E. Palmer, F.R. Spofforth, J.W. Trumble.
(Reinforcements: J. Hardie, H.H. Hyslop).

THE RESULTS

TEST MATCHES	FIRST-CLASS MATCHES	ALL MATCHES
P W L D	P W L D	P W L D
3 0 3 0	37 9 7 21	39 9 8 22

1st Test Manchester: England won by 4 wickets
2nd Test Lord's: England won by an innings and 106 runs
3rd Test The Oval: England won by an innings and 217 runs

1886-87
TOUR OF AUSTRALIA

58 Surrey's George Lohmann dismissed Percy Lewis with the opening ball of the Victoria-England match at Melbourne, thus gaining a wicket with his first delivery in a first-class match in Australia. Lohmann finished the tour-opener with 14 wickets (6-115 & 8-80).

59 On his first-class debut, New South Wales fast bowler J.J. Ferris took 4 for 50 and 3 for 49 against A. Shaw's England XI in November at the SCG. He opened the bowling with Charlie Turner (6-20 & 7-34) – a match-winning combination that secured all 20 wickets.

60 In an odds match at Lithgow in New South Wales, the Englishmen dismissed the local Twenty-Two for 18 and 27, with Johnny Briggs taking 27 for 20 (10-7 & 17-13)!

61 In the first Test match in Sydney, Percy McDonnell became the first captain to win the toss and send in the opposition. J.J. Ferris (4-27) and Charlie Turner (6-15) made their Test debuts and bowled unchanged dismissing England for 45 – their lowest total at Test level. Despite the first-innings collapse, England, with 184, went on to defeat Australia (119 & 97) by 13 runs. Ferris took 5 for 76 in the second innings, and at the age of 19, he remains the youngest Australian bowler to take five wickets in a Test innings. Alec Bannerman (15* & 4) batted for an hour in the second innings without adding to his score, while his brother, Charles, the scorer of the first Test century, made his Test-umpiring debut.

62 Charlie Turner continued to terrorise the English tourists in a first-class match at the SCG in February, taking 14 for 59, including a career-best performance in Australia of 8 for 32. All wickets were obtained without assistance from the field.

63 With Billy Barnes unavailable for the second Test at Sydney – he smashed his hand on a wall after attempting a swipe at Australian captain Percy McDonnell – England acquired the services of Lancashire's Reginald Wood, who, at the time, was playing first-class cricket for Victoria. In his only Test-match appearance, batting at No.10, he scored 6 and 0. George Lohmann became the first bowler to take eight wickets in a Test innings, finishing the match with 10 for 87 (8-35 & 2-52). J.J. Ferris and Charlie Turner took 18 wickets between them, with the latter taking a catch fielding for the opposition.

64 In their first Test series for Australia, J.J. Ferris and Charlie Turner took 35 of the 40 England wickets in the two Tests.

65 William Bruce, the first left-handed batsman selected by Australia to tour England, in 1886, took career-best bowling figures for Victoria against A. Shaw's England XI at the MCG. He opened the batting with scores of 62 and 18 and took 7 for 72 in England's first innings.

66 England's final tour match of the 1886-87 campaign was an encounter billed as 'Smokers v Non-Smokers', played at the East Melbourne Cricket Ground. Each team was a combination of England and local players and the match was drawn. The Non-Smokers batted first and rattled up a new record score in first-class cricket, reaching 803 in about 550 minutes, with England's Arthur Shrewsbury (236) and Victoria's William Bruce (131) adding 196 for the first wicket. In the Smokers' second innings, William Scotton, who had picked up the ball at the end of the match as a souvenir, became the first batsman in Australian first-class cricket to be dismissed 'handled the ball'.

THE TOURISTS

A. Shrewsbury (c), R.G. Barlow, W. Barnes, W. Bates,
J. Briggs, W. Flowers, W. Gunn, J. Lillywhite, G.A. Lohmann,
J.M. Read, W.H. Scotton, A. Shaw.
(Reinforcement: R. Wood).

THE RESULTS

TEST MATCHES	FIRST-CLASS MATCHES	ALL MATCHES
P W L D	P W L D	P W L D
2 2 0 0	10 6 2 2	29 12 2 15

1st Test Sydney: England won by 13 runs
2nd Test Sydney: England won by 71 runs

1887-88
Tour of Australia

67 Two England teams toured Australia in the summer of 1887-88. An Arthur Shrewsbury team was captained by C. Aubrey Smith, who later became a Hollywood film star; the other was led by the Hon. M.B. (later Lord) Hawke, and George Vernon. The two teams, which had arrived in Australia on the same boat, combined to play in the only Test match, at Sydney.

68 The first first-class match by G.F. Vernon's XI, at the Adelaide Oval, was South Australia's first contest on even terms against a touring team. Play was held up for a considerable amount of time, with the umpires and players debating which of the Giffen brothers, Walter or George, should be given out after the stumps had been thrown down. The bails were whipped off as Walter ran towards them, and he headed for the pavilion. It was, however, contended by the England side that they had not crossed, and George should go. The umpires decided Walter was out, and his brother went on to top-score in South Australia's second innings with 81.

69 J.J. Ferris and Charlie Turner continued their dominance over England's batsmen, taking 19 wickets in the match between New South Wales and A. Shrewsbury's England XI at Sydney. In the first innings, Ferris (6-24) was twice on a hat-trick and bowled unchanged with Turner (4-22) dismissing the tourists for a paltry 49. England fared little better second time around, making 66, with Turner claiming 6 for 23 and Ferris 3 for 35. The other wicket was taken by Reginald Allen (1-4), an uncle of England's 'Gubby' Allen.

70 Victoria (68 & 100) sustained its worst-ever defeat in first-class cricket when A. Shrewsbury's England XI (624) gained victory by an innings and 456 runs at the MCG.

71 In the second England match against South Australia, George Giffen (203) scored the first first-class double-century against a touring side. South Australia's Alfred Waldron, in his final first-class match, did not play on the final day due to the death of his child, and appears in the scorebook as 'retired out, 0'.

72 Harry Thorpe, who played district cricket in Sydney, made his only first-class appearance when given the chance to represent an Australian XI against G.F. Vernon's England XI at the MCG. He opened the bowling, without success, recording figures of 0 for 36 in his only first-class innings.

73 In the New South Wales-A. Shrewsbury's England XI match in January at the SCG, an opening bowler from each side claimed 14 wickets. England's George Lohmann took 7 for 68 and 7 for 97, while Charlie Turner recorded the best-ever match-analysis for New South Wales, with 16 for 79 (8-39 & 8-40).

74 Playing for the Combined XI against Arthur Shrewsbury's XI at Sydney, Alec Bannerman (45*) became the second batsman in Australian first-class cricket to carry his bat. The English captain C. Aubrey Smith was run out when a shot from his partner Billy Newham deflected off the bowler, Tom Garrett, onto the stumps.

75 England won the only Test match of 1887-88 by 126 runs. Australia (42 & 82) became the first country in Test cricket to be dismissed for under 100 in both innings – the first-innings effort, their lowest Test total in Australia. Australia's highest individual score in each innings was made by the No.9 batsman. In the first innings, Tom Garrett, with 10, was the only batsman to reach double figures, while the wicket-keeper Jack Blackham top-scored with 25* in the second innings. Australia's Patrick

McShane registered a pair and became the first batsman in Test cricket to make three successive ducks, following a nought in his previous Test innings at Sydney in 1886-87. Charlie Turner took 12 for 87 (5-44 & 7-43), a performance that remains the best bowling in a Test match at the SCG.

76 Charles Bannerman, who had scored Test cricket's first run, ended his first-class career with a duck in the match against G.F. Vernon's XI in Sydney.

77 Representing the A. Shrewsbury England XI at the SCG, George Lohmann (9-67) and Johnny Briggs (11-58) bowled unchanged in each innings to dismiss an Australian XI for 75 and 56.

78 Play was brought to a close at five o'clock on the second day of the Victoria-G.F. Vernon's England XI match at the MCG to accommodate a demonstration Aussie Rules football game between Melbourne and Geelong. The footy certainly enticed the Melbourne crowd, with 9000 spectators turning up, compared to an average audience of 200 for the cricket on the other days.

THE TOURISTS

G.F. Vernon's England team: G.F. Vernon (c), R. Abel, W. Attewell, W. Barnes, J. Beaumont, M.P. Bowden, Lord Hawke, A.E. Newton, T.C. O'Brien, R. Peel, J.T. Rawlin, W.W. Read, A.E. Stoddart.

THE RESULTS

TEST MATCHES*				FIRST-CLASS MATCHES				ALL MATCHES			
P	W	L	D	P	W	L	D	P	W	L	D
1	1	0	0	8	6	1	1	26	11	1	14

A. Shrewsbury's England team: C.A. Smith (c), G. Brann, J. Briggs, L.C. Docker, J. Lillywhite, G.A. Lohmann, W. Newham, R. Pilling, A.D. Pougher, J.M. Preston, J.M. Read, A. Shrewsbury, G. Ulyett.

TEST MATCHES*				FIRST-CLASS MATCHES				ALL MATCHES			
P	W	L	D	P	W	L	D	P	W	L	D
1	1	0	0	7	5	2	0	22	14	2	6

The two teams combined for the only Test match
Only Test Sydney: England won by 126 runs

1888
TOUR OF ENGLAND

79 In the match against Yorkshire at Bradford, George Bonnor scored 115, of which 100 runs came in boundaries (25 fours).

80 Following heavy rain in London, 27 wickets tumbled on the second day on the first Test match at Lord's – the most wickets taken in a single day's Test cricket. Australia (116 & 60) defeated England (53 & 62) by 61 runs, with W.G. Grace's 24, the highest score of the match. Charlie Turner (5-27 & 5-36) took 10 wickets in his first Test match in England.

81 At Hastings, Charlie Turner took 8 for 13 and 9 for 37 against an England XI. His haul of 17 wickets is a record by an Australian bowler in first-class cricket. This was the second occasion on the tour that he'd taken nine in an innings against an England XI, following 9 for 15 at Stoke-on-Trent three weeks earlier.

82 England won both the second and third Tests by an innings margin, with the final match, at Manchester, again affected by heavy rain. On a 'sticky' wicket, Australia (81 & 70) lost 18 wickets before lunch on the second day, a record in all Tests. Following-on, Australia was bundled out in a record time of just 69 minutes. At one stage, Australia was 6 for 7 – the biggest top-order collapse in Test cricket. The first four batsmen made ducks, with eight Australians in the match out for nought – a record number for an Ashes Test. Percy McDonnell and Alec Bannerman were the first pair of openers to score a duck in the same Test innings. The match required only six hours and 34 minutes of playing time and remains the shortest completed Test in England. All three Test matches were completed in two days, a unique occurrence in Test cricket.

83 Percy McDonnell took control of the scoring during the first-class match against Combined Universities Past & Present at Portsmouth, making 69 of the 70 runs added while he was at the wicket.

84 On his first overseas tour, Charlie Turner claimed 283 wickets (average 11.68) and remains the only tourist to take 250 first-class wickets in a season in England. His partner J.J. Ferris took 199 first-class wickets, average 14.74.

THE TOURISTS

P.S. McDonnell (c), A.C. Bannerman, J.McC. Blackham,
G.J. Bonnor, H.F. Boyle, J.D. Edwards, J.J. Ferris,
A.H. Jarvis, S.P. Jones, J.J. Lyons, G.H.S. Trott,
C.T.B. Turner, J. Worrall.
(Reinforcement: S.M.J. Woods).

THE RESULTS

TEST MATCHES	FIRST-CLASS MATCHES	ALL MATCHES
P W L D	P W L D	P W L D
3 1 2 0	37 17 13 7	40 19 14 7

1st Test Lord's: Australia won by 61 runs
2nd Test The Oval: England won by an innings and 137 runs
3rd Test Manchester: England won by an innings and 21 runs

1890
TOUR OF ENGLAND

85 One of the most astounding selections of all time occurred in 1890, when Tasmanian batsman Ken Burn was chosen as Australia's reserve wicket-keeper for the tour of England, even though he had never kept wicket in his life.

86 On his Test debut, at Lord's, Australia's Jack Barrett became the first player to carry his bat in an Ashes Test match, remaining unconquered on 67 in a total of 176, Charlie Turner opened both the bowling and the batting, partnering 'J.J.' Lyons (50 in 36 minutes) in the first innings and Barrett in the second.

87 In the first of only two Test appearances for England, Kent medium-pacer Frederick 'Nutty' Martin opened the bowling against Australia at The Oval with 6 for 50 and 6 for 52 – the first debutant bowler to take 12 wickets in a Test match. Twenty-two wickets fell on the opening day.

88 The Third Test match at Manchester was the first Test abandoned without a ball being bowled.

89 In the first-class match against Lord Londesborough's XI at Scarborough, fast bowler Charlie Turner had the satisfaction of being the top-scoring batsman in each innings (34 & 21). He was also the top wicket-taker in each innings, bowling the Australians to victory, with hauls of 6 for 11 and 7 for 46. Neither side managed to reach 100, with the Lord Londesborough XI dismissed for 39 and 90, the Australians 77 and 60. Johnny Briggs, with 15 for 57, recorded one of first-class cricket's most outstanding bowling performances (9-31 & 6-26) for a player who finished on the losing side.

90 'J.J.' Lyons became the first Australian to be dismissed for 99 in first-class cricket, against the MCC at Lord's. He completed the tour scoring 1029 first-class runs, but at an average of just 17.74.

THE TOURISTS

W.L. Murdoch (c), J.E. Barren, J.McC. Blackham,
E.J.K. Burn, P.C. Charlton, J.J. Ferris, S.E. Gregory,
S.P. Jones, J.J. Lyons, G.H.S. Trott, H. Trumble,
C.T.B. Turner, F.H. Walters.
(Reinforcement: R.J. Pope).

THE RESULTS

TEST MATCHES	FIRST-CLASS MATCHES	ALL MATCHES
P W L D	P W L D	P W L D
2 0 2 0	34 10 16 8	38 13 16 9

1st Test Lord's: England won by 7 wickets
2nd Test The Oval: England won by 2 wickets
3rd Test Manchester: Abandoned

1891-92
Tour of Australia

91 W.G. Grace scored his only first-class century outside of England with a match-winning knock of 159* against Victoria at the MCG. He was the first touring cricketer to carry his bat in a first-class match in Australia.

92 W.G. Grace captained England in his first Test match in Australia, at Melbourne. The first Test of the series drew a crowd of over 60,000 and was the first Test in Australia played over five days. It was also the first Test match in Australia that used six-ball overs.

93 In the second Test at Sydney, Robert Abel (132*) became the first England batsman to carry his bat through a completed Test innings (307). Alec Bannerman whose twin-knocks of 45 and 41 in the first Test took 435 minutes, batted in similarly painstaking fashion at the SCG. His 91 in the second innings was scored in 421 minutes. Johnny Briggs ended Australia's second innings with a hat-trick.

94 England (499) defeated Australia (100 & 169) in the third Test at Adelaide by an innings and 230 runs, the biggest margin of victory in Test cricket to date. Johnny Briggs (6-49 & 6-87) captured 12 of 18 wickets that fell on the third day.

THE TOURISTS
W.G. Grace (c), R. Abel, W. Attewell, G. Bean, J. Briggs,
G.A. Lohmann, G. MacGregor, R. Peel, R. Pilling,
O.G. Radcliffe, J.M. Read, J.W. Sharpe, A.E. Stoddart.

THE RESULTS

TEST MATCHES				FIRST-CLASS MATCHES				ALL MATCHES			
P	W	L	D	P	W	L	D	P	W	L	D
3	1	2	0	8	6	2	0	27	12	2	13

1st Test Melbourne: Australia won by 54 runs
2nd Test Sydney: Australia won by 72 runs
3rd Test Adelaide: England won by an innings and 230 runs

1893
TOUR OF ENGLAND

95 Playing against the MCC at Lord's, 'Affie' Jarvis became the first Australian batsman to be dismissed for a 'king pair' in a first-class match in England.

96 In the first Test at Lord's Arthur Shrewsbury (106) became the first England batsman to score three Test hundreds and the first to reach 1000 runs in Tests between England and Australia. Victorian batsman Harry Graham (107) scored his maiden first-class century in his maiden Test innings. Filling in for an injured W.G. Grace, Andrew Stoddart closed England's second innings at 8 for 234 – the first Test captain to make a declaration. Australia's Jim Phillips became the first umpire to officiate at Test level in two countries.

97 A record eight half-centuries were scored in a single first-class innings by the Australians (843) against Oxford & Cambridge Past & Present at Portsmouth – 'J.J.' Lyons (51), Alec Bannerman (133), 'Harry' Trott (61), Harry Graham (83), William Bruce (191), Hugh Trumble (105), Charlie Turner (66), Walter Giffen (62).

98 In the non-first-class match against Essex at Leyton, Walter Mead created havoc for the Australians, taking 17 wickets for 205 (9-136 & 8-69).

99 Alec Bannerman became the first Australian to score 1000 Test runs during the second Test at The Oval.

THE TOURISTS

J.McC. Blackham (c), A.C. Bannerman, W. Bruce,
A. Coningham, G. Giffen, W.F. Giffen, H. Graham,
S.E. Gregory, A.H. Jarvis, J.J. Lyons, R.W. McLeod,
G.H.S. Trott, H. Trumble, C.T.B. Turner.
(Reinforcement: A.E. Trott).

THE RESULTS

TEST MATCHES				FIRST-CLASS MATCHES				ALL MATCHES			
P	W	L	D	P	W	L	D	P	W	L	D
3	0	1	2	31	14	10	7	36	18	10	8

1st Test Lord's: Drawn
2nd Test The Oval: England won by an innings and 43 runs
3rd Test Manchester: Drawn

1894-95
Tour of Australia

100 In the opening first-class match, at Adelaide, South Australia recorded its first win over an English XI. The victory came via an awesome all-round performance from their captain, George Giffen. With 64 and 58* and 5 for 175 and 6 for 49, he became the first player to score two half-centuries and take five wickets in each innings of a first-class match in Australia. Yorkshire batsman Jack Brown hit 115 in the first innings, to become the first England batsman to score a first-class century on his debut in Australia.

101 In the second tour match, against Victoria, Archie MacLaren (228) became the first batsman to score a double-century in his debut first-class innings in Australia.

102 Bill Howell made his first-class debut for New South Wales, along with future Test players Tom McKibbin and James Kelly, against A.E. Stoddart's XI in Sydney. Howell, who had been selected mainly for his ability with the bat, took five wickets in England's first innings.

103 Queensland suffered an innings-and-274 run thrashing at the Exhibition Ground in Brisbane, in the state's first first-class encounter with an England side. Andrew Stoddart (149) scored the first first-class century against Queensland, while Tom Richardson produced the goods with the ball, taking 8 for 52 and 3 for 11.

104 The first Test match, at the SCG, produced a then-record first-class aggregate of 1514 runs (Australia 586 & 166, England 325 & 437). It was the first Test to involve six playing days and England's 10-run victory provided the first instance of a team winning a Test match after following-on, while Australia became the first country to lose a Test match after scoring 500. Syd Gregory (201) scored the first Test-match double-century in Australia, while George Giffen became the first player to score 200 runs and take eight wickets in an Ashes Test match. Australia's wicket-keeping captain Jack Blackham celebrated his final Test match appearance with a career-best 74, and with Gregory added 154 runs for the ninth wicket, an Australian record in all Tests.

105 The second Test at Melbourne was notable in that for the first time, a wicket fell to the opening delivery. By dismissing England's Archie MacLaren, Arthur Coningham became the first bowler to capture a wicket with his first ball in Test cricket. In England's second innings of 475, all eleven batsmen reached double figures in a Test innings for the first time.

106 On his Test debut, at Adelaide, Australia's Albert Trott scored over 100 runs without being dismissed (38* & 72*) and took eight wickets in an innings. His 8 for 43 remains the best innings return by any bowler on his Test debut. The match was played in extreme heat, with the temperature at one stage reaching 68.3°(C) or 155°(F).

107 In the fourth Test, at the SCG, Andrew Stoddart, the first captain to declare a Test innings closed, became the first England captain to send in the opposition, a decision that ultimately backfired, with Australia gaining victory by an innings and 147 runs. The match remains the shortest Test against England in Australia in terms of balls bowled (908). England's Johnny Briggs became the first bowler to take 100 Test wickets, a feat equalled by Australia's Charlie Turner later in the match. Playing in his final Test, Turner took 3 for 18 and 4 for 33, for a career-total of 101 wickets, average 16.53. Harry Graham scored a century (105) in his first Test in Australia, completing a memorable double, following a century in his maiden Test in England. Yorkshire's Bobby Peel failed with the bat in both innings, becoming the first batsman to record four consecutive Test-match ducks and the first to score two pairs in the same series. He was also the first batsman to be dismissed for a pair in a Test by the same fielding combination (stumped 'Affie' Jarvis, bowled Charlie Turner).

108 The final Test was played at Melbourne, and with the series deadlocked at 2-all, over 100,000 spectators attended a cricket match for the first time in Australia. Albert Trott completed his brief three-match Test career for Australia with a duck, but left with an overall batting average for the country of 102.50. England's John Brown reached 50 in just 28 minutes – the fastest half-century in Ashes cricket – and went on to score a match-winning 140 that gave England the series 3-2. The bat with which Brown scored his century was valued in 1996 at a cool $29,700.

David Frith, the founder and former editor of *Wisden Cricket Monthly*, who purchased the bat for $99 at private sale in 1972, had it valued on a BBC TV program, *Antiques Roadshow*.

109 With 475 runs and 34 wickets, George Giffen became the first cricketer to record the 250 run-20 wicket double in a Test series.

110 Victoria attained its first win in 10 matches against England sides, defeating A.E. Stoddart's XI by seven wickets at the MCG. 'Harry' Trott, the captain and opening batsman, took 8 for 63 and 2 for 74.

111 In the final tour match, at Adelaide, George Giffen (5-309) became the first bowler in first-class cricket to concede 300 runs in an innings. Clem Hill (150*) hit his maiden first-class century, and, at the time, the 18-year-old was the youngest batsman to score a hundred in Australian first-class cricket. Albert Ward, who was England's highest run-scorer in the five-match Test series (419 at 41.90), scored the first double-century against South Australia (219).

THE TOURISTS

A.E. Stoddart (c), J. Briggs, W. Brockwell, J.T. Brown,
F.G.J. Ford, L.H. Gay, W.A. Humphreys, W.H. Lockwood,
A.C. MacLaren, R. Peel, H. Philipson, T. Richardson,
A. Ward.

THE RESULTS

TEST MATCHES	FIRST-CLASS MATCHES	ALL MATCHES
P W L D	P W L D	P W L D
5 3 2 0	12 8 4 0	23 9 4 10

1st Test Sydney: England won by 10 runs
2nd Test Melbourne: England won by 94 runs
3rd Test Adelaide: Australia won by 382 runs
4th Test Sydney: Australia won by an innings and 147 runs
5th Test Melbourne: England won by 6 wickets

1896
Tour of England

112 The Australians were dismissed for 18 at Lord's by the MCC, their lowest total in first-class cricket. Leicestershire all-rounder Dick Pougher took a record five wickets without conceding a run.

113 Two wicket-keepers – Australia's James Kelly and England's 'Dick' Lilley – made their Test debuts at Lord's, and both made a first-innings duck. The first Test of a three-match series marked the final appearance of Surrey match-winner George Lohmann. In 18 Tests, Lohmann took 112 wickets, average 10.75.

114 The second Test at Manchester saw the first appearance in the England XI of K.S. Ranjitsinhji, the first Indian to play Test cricket. 'Ranji' scored a century (154*) in the second innings, becoming the first batsman to make a hundred runs before lunch in a Test match. George Giffen, who played all of his 31 Tests against England, became the first cricketer to reach the Test double of 1000 runs and 100 wickets.

115 England won the final match at The Oval, and the series 2-1, with Bobby Peel taking 6 for 23 in his final Test innings. Australia was dismissed for 44 in the second innings, with Tom McKibbin (16), batting at No.11, the only batsman to reach double figures.

116 Gloucestershire, with 17, incurred the lowest first-class total for an English county against an Australian side, at Cheltenham. Hugh Trumble (6-8) and Tom McKibbin (4-7) were the destroyers.

THE TOURISTS

G.H.S. Trott (c), J. Darling, H. Donnan, C.J. Eady,
G. Giffen, H. Graham, S.E. Gregory, C. Hill, F.A. Iredale,
A.E. Johns, E. Jones, J.J. Kelly, T.R. McKibbin, H. Trumble.

THE RESULTS

TEST MATCHES	FIRST-CLASS MATCHES	ALL MATCHES
P W L D	P W L D	P W L D
3 1 2 0	34 20 6 8	34 20 6 8

1st Test Lord's: England won by 6 wickets
2nd Test Manchester: Australia won by 3 wickets
3rd Test The Oval: England won by 66 runs

1897-98
TOUR OF AUSTRALIA

117 Opening the batting against New South Wales at the SCG, Archie MacLaren (142 & 100) became the first English player to score a century in each innings of a first-class match in Australia. A month later, MacLaren scored 109* in the first Test match at the SCG, in his first Test as captain, and became the first batsman to score centuries in three successive first-class innings in Australia. K.S. Ranjitsinhji (175) scored his second successive first-class hundred on tour, and joined Harry Graham in scoring a century in his first Test in both England and Australia. Joe Darling opened Australia's second innings with 101 – the first left-handed batsman to score a Test century. James Kelly became the first wicket-keeper not to allow a bye in a Test-match total exceeding 500. Clem Hill scored 96 in the second innings, the first of five nineties he would make in Tests against England.

118 In the second Test match at Melbourne, Australia's Ernie Jones became the first bowler to be no-balled for throwing in Test cricket. The umpire who made the historic call was Jim Phillips. Charlie McLeod, who was dismissed in unusual circumstances in the previous Test – he was bowled by a no-ball, left the crease and was run out – scored a century, Australia's first at the MCG since 1881-82. Australia made 520 and won the match by an innings and 55 runs.

119 Joe Darling became the first batsman to score two centuries in the same Test series, when he opened with 178 in the third Test at Adelaide. His hundred was reached with a six, another first. Darling's contribution formed part of a mammoth match-winning total of 573, Australia becoming the first side to score 500 in successive Test innings.

120 In the fourth Test at Melbourne, Clem Hill made the highest score by an under-21 player in Ashes cricket with a knock of 188. He was 20 years and 317 days old. With Hugh Trumble (46), he shared a 165-run partnership for the seventh wicket, a record for that wicket against England.

121 The tour match between England and New South Wales at Sydney in February produced 1739 runs, with 14 half-centuries. The NSW No.11 Bill Howell enjoyed a remarkable match, scoring 48 in the first innings and 95 in the second.

122 Joe Darling (160) reached 100, with 80 runs in boundaries, in just 91 minutes in the fifth Test at Sydney, becoming the first batsman to score three centuries in a Test series and the first to exceed 500 in a rubber. Tom Richardson took a Test-best 8 for 94 in his final appearance, and finished the match with the fourth ten-wicket haul of his career, a record for an England bowler against Australia.

123 Tom Richardson conceded over 100 runs five times in six consecutive innings during the series – 2-121 in the first Test at Sydney, 1-114 in the second Test at Melbourne, 4-164 at Adelaide, 2-102 at the MCG and 8-94 & 2-110 at the SCG.

124 During the first innings of the match against Victoria at the MCG, Archie MacLaren and K.S. Ranjitsinhji became the first touring players to score 1000 runs in an Australian first-class season.

THE TOURISTS

A.E. Stoddart (c), J.H. Board, J. Briggs, N.F. Druce,
T. Hayward, J.T. Hearne, G.H. Hirst, A.C. MacLaren,
J.R. Mason, K.S. Ranjitsinhji, T. Richardson, W. Storer,
E. Wainwright.

THE RESULTS

TEST MATCHES				FIRST-CLASS MATCHES				ALL MATCHES			
P	W	L	D	P	W	L	D	P	W	L	D
5	1	4	0	12	4	5	3	22	6	5	11

1st Test Sydney: England won by 9 wickets
2nd Test Melbourne: Australia won by an innings and 55 runs
3rd Test Adelaide: Australia won by an innings and 13 runs
4th Test Melbourne: Australia won by 8 wickets
5th Test Sydney: Australia won by 6 wickets

1899
Tour of England

125 In his first first-class match in England, Bill Howell returned Australia's best first-class bowling figures taking 10 for 28 against Surrey (114) at The Oval – eight of his victims were bowled. He also took 5 for 29 in the second innings.

126 W.G. Grace made his final England appearance in the first Test at Nottingham and was 50 years and 320 days old at the completion of the match. He remains Test cricket's oldest captain, with only Wilfred Rhodes, who made his debut in this match, playing Test cricket for England at a greater age. Victor Trumper also made his Test debut here, marking his first appearance with a duck.

127 During the first-class match against Cambridge University, Australian bowlers Ernie Jones (5) and Bill Howell (4, 4, 4, 4) combined to score a world-record 21 runs off a five-ball over from Rockley Wilson.

128 Two batsmen scored hundreds in the second Test at Lord's, both reaching 135. Clem Hill was one, the other was the 21-year-old Victor Trumper, who remained undefeated in his first Test appearance at the home of cricket.

129 Jack Hearne took one of Test cricket's most celebrated hat-tricks in the third match at Leeds, dismissing three of Australia's best batsmen – Clem Hill, Syd Gregory and Monty Noble – for ducks.

130 'Bill' Bradley took 5 for 67 on his Test debut at Old Trafford, including a wicket with his first delivery – the first instance of such a feat by an England bowler. Monty Noble, with 60 and 89*, became the first batsman to score two half-centuries on the same day in a Test match.

131 Victor Trumper scored a chanceless 300* against Sussex at Hove, the highest innings of the tour. It was the first triple-century scored by an Australian in England.

132 Charlie Llewellyn, the South African Test all-rounder, made his first-class debut for Hampshire in 1899 in the match against the Australians at Southampton. He scored 72 and took 8 for 132 in the second innings – the best bowling performance by a debutant in a first-class match for Hampshire.

133 England's first five-match Test series, won by Australia 1-0, ended at The Oval with F.S. Jackson (118) and Tom Hayward (137) scoring 185 for the first wicket – the first pair of openers to score centuries in the same Test innings.

134 Representing C.I. Thornton's XI at Scarborough, Wilfred Rhodes took 9 for 24 in the Australians' second-innings total of 83, with seven wickets coming in 24 balls.

THE TOURISTS

J. Darling (c), S.E. Gregory, C. Hill, W.P. Howell, F.A. Iredale, A.E. Johns, E. Jones, J.J. Kelly, F.J. Laver, C.E. McLeod, M.A. Noble, H. Trumble, V.T. Trumper, J. Worrall.

THE RESULTS

TEST MATCHES	FIRST-CLASS MATCHES	ALL MATCHES
P W L D	P W L D	P W L D
5 1 0 4	35 16 3 16	35 16 3 16

1st Test Nottingham: Drawn
2nd Test Lord's: Australia won by 10 wickets
3rd Test Leeds: Drawn
4th Test Manchester: Drawn
5th Test The Oval: Drawn

1901-1912

1901-02
Tour Of Australia

135 In England's first first-class match of the 1901-02 tour, at Adelaide, George Giffen recorded the best innings-figures by a South Australian against an English XI (7-46) and his best match figures for the state, taking 13 for 93. Clem Hill was the only batsman to score a fifty in the match, with 107 and 80.

136 England won the first Test at the SCG by an innings and 124 runs, with all 20 wickets taken by debutants. Three bowlers whose surnames began with the letter 'B' dominated proceedings, with openers Len Braund and Sydney Barnes taking seven and six wickets respectively, and 'Charlie' Blythe seven. England's skipper Archie MacLaren made 116, becoming the first batsman to score four Test centuries.

137 Twenty-five wickets fell on the opening day of the second Test at Melbourne, a record number in Australia. In the second innings Clem Hill became the first batsman to score 99 in a Test match, while Reggie Duff, with 104 on his debut, remains the only batsman to score a century at No.10 against England. Duff and Warwick Armstrong (45*) recorded the first century tenth-wicket partnership in Test cricket. Hugh Trumble, who opened the batting with Joe Darling in the second innings, completed an Australian victory by taking a hat-trick with the last three balls of the match.

138 Clem Hill followed his 99 at Melbourne with 98 and 97 in the third Test at Adelaide, becoming the first batsman to score three successive Test-match nineties. For the first time, over 300 runs were scored in the fourth innings to win a Test, with Australia reaching 315 to claim victory by four wickets.

139 Despite posting a healthy total of 432 against A.C. MacLaren's XI at Sydney, New South Wales lost the match by an innings and 128 runs. After the visitors made 769 – the highest total by a touring team in Australia – NSW was bowled out for 209 in its second innings. The home-side's 432 is the highest score in Australian first-class cricket for a team losing by an innings margin.

140 Batting at No.10 in the fourth Test at Sydney, Australia's Bill Howell scored 35 in 14 minutes off 15 balls. Team-mate James Kelly took four catches in each innings, becoming the first wicket-keeper to achieve eight dismissals in a Test match. Victorian bowler Jack Saunders took nine wickets on his Test debut.

141 Clem Hill came close, once again, to scoring his first hundred of the series, in the final Test at Melbourne, only to be dismissed for 87 – Australia's 'hoodoo' number. He became the first batsman to score 500 runs in a Test series without a century.

THE TOURISTS

A.C. MacLaren (c), S.F. Barnes, C. Blythe, L.C. Braund,
H.G. Garnett, J. Gum, T. Hayward, G.L. Jessop, A.O. Jones,
A.F.A. Lilley, C.P. McGahey, W.G. Quaife, E. Robson,
J.T. Tyldesley.

THE RESULTS

TEST MATCHES	FIRST-CLASS MATCHES	ALL MATCHES
P W L D	P W L D	P W L D
5 1 4 0	1 5 6 0	22 8 6 8

1st Test Sydney: England won by an innings and 124 runs
2nd Test Melbourne: Australia won by 229 runs
3rd Test Adelaide: Australia won by 4 wickets
4th Test Sydney: Australia won by 7 wickets
5th Test Melbourne: Australia won by 32 runs

1902
TOUR OF ENGLAND

142 Australia was dismissed for 36 in 23 overs, by George Hirst (3-15) and Wilfred Rhodes (7-17), in the first Test match to be staged at Edgbaston. Victor Trumper (18) was the only batsman to reach double figures in a total that remains Australia's lowest score in Tests.

143 In the following match at Headingley, Yorkshire defeated the Australians by five wickets, thanks to the bowling of F.S. Jackson (4-30 & 5-12) and George Hirst (4-35 & 5-9). Australia was bowled out for 23 in the second innings, their lowest total against an English county. Jackson took four wickets in five balls, the first example of such a feat by an England bowler against Australia.

144 Australia's Bert Hopkins gained his only two Test wickets of the tour in sensational style in the washed-out second Test at Lord's. Opening the bowling, he disposed of C.B. Fry and K.S. Ranjitsinhji, both for ducks, without conceding a run in his first two overs.

145 Sheffield hosted its first and only Test match at Bramall Lane, where Clem Hill recorded the ground's only Test century (119) and Monty Noble the only ten-wicket haul (11-103).

146 In the match against Surrey at The Oval, Australia's Clem Hill scored nine runs off one ball bowled by Tom Richardson. He scored 7, 8 and 9 off three balls in two overs.

147 In the fourth Test at Manchester, Victor Trumper (104) became the first batsman to score a Test century before lunch on the first day. His opening partnership of 135 with Reggie Duff took just 78 minutes, with the hundred posted in 57. In his first-innings knock of 51, Joe Darling scored the first two sixes hit out of the ground in a Test match in England.

148 England won the final Test at The Oval by the narrowest of margins – the first one-wicket victory in Test cricket. Hugh Trumble became the first Australian to score a half-century and take 10 wickets in a Test with 64* and 8 for 65 and 4 for 108. Gilbert Jessop propelled England to victory scoring 104, his 50 coming in 43 minutes, his 100 in 75 – the fastest hundred in an Ashes Test match.

149 Victor Trumper was the first Australian batsman to score 2000 first-class runs in an English season. His tally of 2570 runs, average 48.49, included 11 centuries. Two of those hundreds (109 & 119) came in the match against Essex at Leyton, the first instance of an Australian scoring a century in each innings of a first-class match in England.

THE TOURISTS

J. Darling (c), W.W. Armstrong, H. Carter, R.A. Duff,
S.E. Gregory, C. Hill, A.J.Y. Hopkins, W.P. Howell, E. Jones,

J.J. Kelly, M.A. Noble, J.V. Saunders, H. Trumble, V.T. Trumper. (Reinforcement: R.J. Pope).

THE RESULTS

TEST MATCHES	FIRST-CLASS MATCHES	ALL MATCHES
P W L D	P W L D	P W L D
5 2 1 2	37 21 2 14	39 23 2 14

1st Test Birmingham: Drawn
2nd Test Lord's: Drawn
3rd Test Bramall Lane: Australia won by 143 runs
4th Test Manchester: Australia won by 3 runs
5th Test The Oval: England won by 1 wicket

1902-03
Tour of Australia

150 After completing a tour of New Zealand, an England team led by Lord Hawke played three matches against the Sheffield Shield states, Victoria, New South Wales and South Australia. Victoria won its match at the MCG, with Harry Graham top-scoring with 92 in his final innings for the state.

151 In the match against Lord Hawke's England XI at Unley Oval in Adelaide, medium-pacer Harry Hay, a late replacement, made history becoming the first bowler to capture a hat-trick on his first-class debut in Australia. He took 9 for 67 in the second innings, the best first-class bowling performance against England in Australia, while George Thompson, with 9 for 85, recorded the best bowling performance by an English player in Australia.

THE TOURISTS

P.F. Warner (c), B.J.T. Bosanquet, C.J. Burnup, E.M. Dowson,
F.L. Fane, S. Hargreave, P.R Johnson, A.E. Leatham,
J. Stanning, T.L. Taylor, G.J. Thompson, A.D. Whatmore.

THE RESULTS

FIRST-CLASS MATCHES				ALL MATCHES			
P	W	L	D	P	W	L	D
3	0	2	1	3	0	2	1

1903-04
TOUR OF AUSTRALIA

152 This was the first tour by England under the auspices of the MCC. 'Tip' Foster made 287 in the first Test at Sydney, the highest innings by a batsman on his Test debut. He was also the first batsman to take part in three century stands in one Test innings, his tenth-wicket partnership of 130 with Wilfred Rhodes, an Ashes record. Monty Noble scored his only Test-match century (133) in his first Test as captain.

153 In the second Test at the MCG, Wilfred Rhodes became the first England bowler to take 15 wickets in a Test match against Australia. England's Bert Strudwick became the first substitute fielder to take three catches in a Test innings. In Australia's second innings of 111, every batsman was caught, a first in Test cricket.

154 Clem Hill became the first batsman to score 2000 Test runs during the third Test at Adelaide. With 113, Victor Trumper became the first batsman to score four Test centuries against England and for the fourth time in successive Test innings in this rubber, he top-scored for Australia. In the second innings, Syd Gregory (112) emulated Trumper's feat of four Test hundreds v England.

155 In a match against Tasmania at Launceston, the MCC provided the first occasion in Australian first-class cricket of all eleven players bowling in an innings.

156 At the Melbourne Cricket Ground, the MCC dismissed Victoria in the second innings for 15 – the lowest innings total in Australian first-class cricket. Wilfred Rhodes, with 5 for 6, dismissed Percy McAlister and Warwick Armstrong with successive deliveries in the opening over, and was unlucky to see 'Harry' Trott put down next ball. Ted Arnold (4-8) repeated his partner's feat of taking wickets with his first two deliveries, reducing Victoria to four wickets down with no runs on the board.

157 A player with one of the longest names in the game, John Elicius Benedict Bernard Placid Quirk Carrington Dwyer, acted as 12th man for New South Wales against the MCC in Sydney. Dwyer, a Sydney-born fast bowler with the Glebe club, later went to England and played first-class cricket for Sussex (1904-09).

158 The fourth Test at the SCG was a low-scoring affair that spanned six days, with repeated interruptions due to rain. Bernard Bosanquet took 5 for 12 and finished with 6 for 52, with England regaining the Ashes.

159 Eleven ducks were scored in the fifth Test at Melbourne. Hugh Trumble, in his final first-class appearance became the first bowler to take two Test-match hat-tricks.

160 England's 'Dick' Lilley made at least one stumping in each of five Tests, finishing with nine – a record for an Ashes series.

THE TOURISTS

P.F. Warner (c), E.G. Arnold, B.J.T. Bosanquet, L.C. Braund,
A. Fielder, R.E. Foster, T. Hayward, G.H. Hirst, A.E. Knight,
A.F.A. Lilley, A.E. Relf, W. Rhodes, H. Strudwick,
J.T. Tyldesley.

THE RESULTS

TEST MATCHES	FIRST-CLASS MATCHES	ALL MATCHES
P W L D	P W L D	P W L D
5 3 2 0	14 9 2 3	20 10 2 8

1st Test Sydney: England won by 5 wickets
2nd Test Melbourne: England won by 185 runs
3rd Test Adelaide: Australia won by 216 runs
4th Test Sydney: England won by 157 runs
5th Test Melbourne: Australia won by 218 runs

AUSTRALIA VERSUS ENGLAND 1861-2005

1905
TOUR OF ENGLAND

161 Bernard Bosanquet, who bowled England to victory in the fourth Test at Sydney in 1903-04, bowled another match-winning spell in the first Test at Nottingham. His 8 for 107 was the finest of his short England career. Archie MacLaren scored 140 in the second innings, becoming the first batsman to score five Test centuries. The two captains for this series, F.S. Jackson and Joe Darling, were both born on the same day – 21 November 1870.

162 In the third Test in Leeds, F.S. Jackson (144*) scored the first Test hundred at Headingley, and made another (113) in his next innings at Old Trafford, becoming the first batsman to record five Test centuries in England.

163 During the tour match against at Worcestershire, 'Tibby' Cotter performed one of the greatest spells of wicket-taking in first-class cricket by taking seven wickets in 28 balls.

164 In the final Test at The Oval, F.S. Jackson crowned a memorable series by becoming the first captain to win every toss in a five-match rubber. England retained the Ashes under Jackson's captaincy, while on a personal note, he topped both the batting and bowling averages. With a first-innings knock of 146, Reggie Duff became the first batsman to score a century in both his first and last Tests between Australia and England. Arthur Jones was the first substitute to keep wicket in a Test match, and was the first to make a dismissal, when he caught Warwick Armstrong.

THE TOURISTS

J. Darling (c), W.W. Armstrong, A. Cotter, R.A. Duff,
D.R.A. Gehrs, S.E. Gregory, C. Hill, A.J.Y. Hopkins,
W.P. Howell, J.J. Kelly, F.J. Laver, C.E. McLeod,
P.M. Newland, M.A. Noble, V.T. Trumper.

THE RESULTS

TEST MATCHES	FIRST-CLASS MATCHES	ALL MATCHES
P W L D	P W L D	P W L D
5 0 2 3	35 15 3 17	38 16 3 19

1st Test Nottingham: England won by 213 runs
2nd Test Lord's: Drawn
3rd Test Leeds: Drawn
4th Test Manchester: England won by an innings and 80 runs
5th Test The Oval: Drawn

1907-08
Tour of Australia

165 Western Australia played its first first-class match against an international side at the WACA in 1907-08. The MCC won by an innings, with opening batsman Frederick Fane (133) scoring the first hundred by an England batsman in Western Australia.

166 While scoring 8 declared for 660 against South Australia at Adelaide, four of the MCC batsmen made centuries – Arthur Jones (119), Joseph Hardstaff (135), Len Braund (160) and Jack Crawford (114).

167 George Gunn, who had been convalescing in Australia, was included as a late replacement in England's line-up for the first Test at Sydney and top-scored (119 & 74) in each innings, becoming the fifth England batsman to make a hundred on his debut.

168 Jack Hobbs made his England debut in the second Test at Melbourne scoring 100 runs (83 & 28). Kenneth Hutchings (126), in his second Test, scored his sole Test century. The match went right down to the wire, and had Gerry Hazlitt hit the stumps with an accurate throw while the winning run was being taken, this match would have ended in Test cricket's first tie.

169 Roger Hartigan (116) scored a century on his debut, in the third Test at Adelaide, setting an Australian record eighth-wicket partnership against all countries of 243 with Clem Hill (160), who made the highest Test score by an Australian No.9 batsman.

170 Victor Trumper made a pair in the fourth Test at Melbourne, while Warwick Armstrong (133*) scored his first century against England. Jack Hobbs scored his first Test-duck in the second innings as England pursued a target of 495. Australia won the match, and the Ashes.

171 In the fifth Test at Sydney, Victor Trumper (166) followed his two ducks at Melbourne with his fifth hundred against England, becoming the second batsman, after Clem Hill, to pass 2000 Test runs.

172 Len Braund and Jack Crawford both appeared in 16 first-class matches on tour, and each completed the double of 500 runs and 50 wickets. The two were the first tourists to secure the all-round feat in Australian first-class cricket. Braund scored 783 runs and took 50 wickets, his team-mate 610 runs and 66 wickets.

THE TOURISTS

A.O. Jones (c), S.F. Barnes, C. Blythe, L.C. Braund,
J.N. Crawford, F.L. Lane, A. Fielder, J. Hardstaff Snr,
E.G. Hayes, J.B. Hobbs, J. Humphries, I.C.L. Hutchings,
W. Rhodes, R.A. Young.
(Reinforcement: G. Gunn).

THE RESULTS

TEST MATCHES	FIRST-CLASS MATCHES	ALL MATCHES
P W L D	P W L D	P W L D
5 1 4 0	18 7 4 7	19 7 4 8

1st Test Sydney: Australia won by 2 wickets
2nd Test Melbourne: England won by 1 wicket
3rd Test Adelaide: Australia won by 245 runs
4th Test Melbourne: Australia won by 308 runs
5th Test Sydney: Australia won by 49 runs

1909
TOUR OF ENGLAND

173 In the first Test at Edgbaston, George Hirst and 'Charlie' Blythe shared all 20 Australian wickets to win the match by 10 wickets. The pair both took 5 for 58 in the second innings. Jack Hobbs and C.B. Fry, who were both dismissed first-ball by Charles Macartney in the first innings, shared an unbroken stand of 105 in the second, guiding England to a comfortable victory.

174 Charles Macartney took a career-best 7 for 58 and 10 wickets in the third Test at Leeds. In the following Test at Manchester, a 39-year-old Frank Laver took 8 for 31, the best innings figures by an Australian in a Test match in England.

175 In the final Test at The Oval, Monty Noble became the first Australian captain to win all five tosses in a series. Australia's Warren Bardsley (136 & 130) became the first batsman to score a century in each innings of a Test match.

THE TOURISTS

M.A. Noble (c), W.W. Armstrong, W. Bardsley, W. Carkeek,
A. Cotter, S.E. Gregory, M.J. Hartigan, A.J.Y. Hopkins,
F.J. Laver, P.A. McAlister, J.D.A. O'Connor, V.S. Ransford,
V.T. Trumper, W.J. Whitty.

THE RESULTS

TEST MATCHES				FIRST-CLASS MATCHES				ALL MATCHES			
P	W	L	D	P	W	L	D	P	W	L	D
5	2	1	2	37	11	4	22	39	13	4	22

1st Test Birmingham: England won by 10 wickets
2nd Test Lord's: Australia won by 9 wickets
3rd Test Leeds: Australia won by 126 runs
4th Test Manchester: Drawn
5th Test The Oval: Drawn

1911-12
TOUR OF AUSTRALIA

176 In the first-class tour match against South Australia at Adelaide, nine different local batsmen were dismissed for a duck.

177 J.W.H.T. Douglas, the England captain, scored 33* in 189 minutes against Victoria, an innings that gave birth to his famous nickname, 'Johnny Won't Hit Today'.

178 'Ranji' Hordern, the New South Wales googly bowler, marked his first appearance in a Test match against England by taking 12 wickets (5-85 & 7-90) at Sydney. Victor Trumper (113) scored his eighth century at Test level, and his sixth against England. When Clem Hill (65) reached 45 in the second innings, he became the first batsman to pass 10,000 first-class runs in Australia.

179 Sydney Barnes destroyed Australia's hopes in the second Test at Melbourne, taking a wicket with the first ball of the match and 4 for 1 in his opening spell. 'Young Jack' Hearne (114), at the age of 20 years 324 days, became the youngest England batsman to score a century in Australia.

180 In the third Test, Jack Hobbs became the first batsman to score 300 runs without being dismissed in Test cricket. After scoring an unbeaten 126 in the second innings at Melbourne, Hobbs then made 187 at the Adelaide Oval, the highest of his 12 Test tons against Australia.

181 Frank Woolley scored an unbeaten 305 for the MCC at Hobart, the highest first-class innings in Tasmania. He reached 300 in just 219 minutes and shared in two double-century partnerships.

182 Jack Hobbs (178) and Wilfred Rhodes (179) opened England's innings in the fourth Test at Melbourne with 323, England's highest partnership for any wicket in Australia.

183 Following his 179 at Melbourne, Wilfred Rhodes scored a pair of centuries (119 & 109) in the match against New South Wales, becoming only the second England tourist, after Archie MacLaren, to score three consecutive first-class hundreds in Australia.

184 The fifth Test at Sydney was the first Test to last seven days, although two days were lost to rain. Frank Woolley hit an unconquered 133, becoming the first left-handed England batsman to score a century against Australia. Later in the match, Woolley recorded an unusual bowling analysis, taking more wickets than he conceded runs (2-1-1-2). Victor Trumper and Clem Hill, at the time Australia's highest run-scorers, both made their final Test appearances.

185 Sydney Barnes took 59 first-class wickets, average 20.86, and at 38 years 300 days on the final day of his last match on tour, he is the oldest bowler to take 50 wickets in an Australian season.

THE TOURISTS

P.F. Warner (c), S.F. Barnes, J.W.H.T. Douglas, F.R. Foster, G. Gunn, J.W. Hearne, J.W. Hitch, J.B. Hobbs, J. Iremonger, S. Kinnier, C.P. Mead, W. Rhodes, E.J. Smith, H. Strudwick, J. Vine, F.E. Woolley.

THE RESULTS

TEST MATCHES				FIRST-CLASS MATCHES				ALL MATCHES			
P	W	L	D	P	W	L	D	P	W	L	D
5	4	1	0	14	11	1	2	18	12	1	5

1st Test Sydney: Australia won by 146 runs
2nd Test Melbourne: England won by 8 wickets
3rd Test Adelaide: England won by 7 wickets
4th Test Melbourne: England won by an innings and 225 runs
5th Test Sydney: England won by 70 runs

1912
TOUR OF ENGLAND

186 Australia and South Africa toured England in 1912 to compete in Test cricket's first triangular Test series. Due to a dispute with the Australian Board of Control over the organisation and financial management of tours to and from Australia, no less than six of the country's leading players, Clem Hill, Victor Trumper, Warwick Armstrong, 'Tibby' Cotter, 'Sammy' Carter and Vernon Ransford, refused to go.

187 In Australia's first Test of the series against England, at Lord's, Charles Macartney became the first batsman to score 99 in a Test match in England. The third England-Australia Test, at The Oval, was the first timeless Test match in England. Australia lost nine wickets for 19 in the second innings, dismissed for just 65, England gaining victory by 244 runs. Frank Woolley scored a half-century and took 10 wickets.

THE TOURISTS

S.E. Gregory (c), W. Bardsley, W. Carkeek, S.H. Emery, G.R. Hazlitt, C.B. Jennings, C. Kelleway, C.G. Macartney, J.W. McLaren, T.J. Matthew, R.E. Mayne, R.B. Minnett, D.B.M. Smith, H. Webster, W.J. Whitty.

THE RESULTS

TEST MATCHES	FIRST-CLASS MATCHES	ALL MATCHES
P W L D	P W L D	P W L D
3 0 1 2	36 9 8 19	37 9 8 20

1st Test Lord's: Drawn
2nd Test Manchester: Drawn
3rd Test The Oval: England won by 244 runs

1919-1938

1919
TOUR OF ENGLAND

188 With the First World War at an end, the first cricket team to undertake an overseas tour was the Australian Imperial Forces team. Four batsmen passed 1000 first-class runs on the tour, with Herbie Collins reaching the double of 1000 runs and 100 wickets. Jack Gregory took 100 wickets in his debut first-class season, snaring 131 scalps, average 18.19. The highest individual score during the summer was 195* by 'Nip' Pellew against Worcestershire, while the best bowling was an innings-haul of 9 for 42 by 'Ally' Lampard against Lancashire. In the match against Surrey at The Oval, Pellew (106*) and Lampard (112) scored 170 for the seventh wicket. At Cambridge, the University pair of Gerald Rotherham (84*) and John Naumann (51) put on 145 for the tenth wicket – the highest last-wicket stand against an Australian team in first-class cricket.

THE TOURISTS

H.L. Collins (c), E.A. Bull, C.T. Docker, J.M. Gregory, H.F.T. Heath, C. Kelleway, A.W. Lampard, E.J. Long, H.S.B. Love, J.T. Murray, W.A.S. Oldfield, C.E. Pellew, W.S. Stirling, J.M. Taylor, W.L. Trenerry, C.B. Willis, C.S. Winning.

THE RESULTS

FIRST-CLASS MATCHES				ALL MATCHES			
P	W	L	D	P	W	L	D
28	12	4	12	32	13	4	15

1920-21
Tour of Australia

189 In England's first first-class match in Australia since 1911-12, the MCC posted a total of 5 declared for 512 against South Australia. The English batsmen recorded a century partnership for the first three wickets, a feat they repeated in their next innings, against Victoria at the MCG.

190 In his first first-class match in Australia, Jack Gregory, on his New South Wales debut, took nine wickets against the MCC in Sydney.

191 Warwick Armstrong began his highly successful term as Australian captain scoring a century (158) in the first Test at Sydney. Herbie Collins (104) also scored a hundred, on his Test debut, and at the age of 31, was the oldest to do so. With 70 in the first innings, Collins became the first Australian to begin his Test career with a century and a half-century in his first match. Wilfred Rhodes became the first England player to reach the Test double of 2000 runs and 100 wickets. There were six run-outs in this match, five by Australia and one by England.

192 Roy Park replaced an ill Charles Macartney for the second Test at Melbourne, and made a first-ball duck in his only Test innings. 'Nip' Pellew and Jack Gregory both scored centuries in their second Test. Later in the match, Gregory took 7 for 69, becoming the first player in Ashes history to score a century and take five wickets in an innings.

193 Six centuries were scored for the first time in a Test match, at Adelaide. Warwick Armstrong (121) scored the 100th century in Australia-England Tests in Australia's second-innings total of 582. This remains the highest-scoring Ashes Test on record, the match producing 1753 runs. Arthur Mailey gained his first ten-wicket haul in Test cricket, taking 5 for 160 and 5 for 142, becoming the first bowler to concede 300 runs in a Test. In the fourth match at Melbourne, Mailey claimed 13 wickets and provided the first example of an Australian bowler taking nine wickets in a Test innings (9-121).

194 In the New South Wales-MCC match at Sydney, Johnny Douglas scored 100 runs (46 & 82*) and took a hat-trick.

AUSTRALIA VERSUS ENGLAND 1861-2005

195 Australia won the final Test match at Sydney by nine wickets, completing an emphatic and unprecedented 5-0 series victory. Jack Gregory became the first fielder to take 15 catches in a Test series. Arthur Mailey took 36 wickets in his first Test series, at the time a record number for an Australian in a five-match rubber against England. Twenty-seven half-centuries were scored by Australian batsmen during the series, while England's batsmen made 22. The total of 49 fifties is a record for an Ashes series.

THE TOURISTS

J.W.H.T. Douglas (c), A. Dolphin, P.G.H. Fender,
J.W. Hearne, E.H. Hendren, J.W. Hitch, J.B. Hobbs,
H. Howell, J.W.H. Makepeace, C.H. Parkin, W. Rhodes,
C.A.G. Russell, H. Strudwick, A. Waddington, E.R. Wilson,
F.E. Woolley.

THE RESULTS

TEST MATCHES	FIRST-CLASS MATCHES	ALL MATCHES
P W L D	P W L D	P W L D
5 0 5 0	13 5 6 2	22 9 6 7

1st Test Sydney: Australia won by 377 runs
2nd Test Melbourne: Australia won by an innings and 91 runs
3rd Test Adelaide: Australia won by 119 runs
4th Test Melbourne: Australia won by 8 wickets
5th Test Sydney: Australia won by 9 wickets

1921
TOUR OF ENGLAND

196 The first Test at Nottingham was the 100th between the two countries. Australia's new pair of fast-bowling openers, Ted McDonald and Jack Gregory, took 16 wickets between them.

197 In the second Test at Lord's, Frank Woolley (95 & 93) became the first England batsman to score two nineties in the same Test match. England introduced four new Test players, following five debutants in the first Test.

198 Between the second and third Tests, the Australians scored over 500 in three successive first-class innings against county sides – 621 v Northamptonshire at Northampton, 675 v Nottinghamshire at Trent Bridge and 506 v Warwickshire at Birmingham.

199 Charles Macartney made the highest first-class score by an Australian batsman in England with an innings of 345 in 232 minutes in the match against Nottinghamshire. All of his runs came on the first day, a record for an Australian batsman in first-class cricket. He reached 300 in 198 minutes, the fastest triple-century by an Australian in first-class cricket.

200 England suffered its eighth consecutive Test-match defeat, all of them against Australia, at Leeds. Charles Macartney (115) scored his fourth consecutive first-class century of the tour, his hundred here being the first by an Australian in a Test at Leeds.

201 There was an unusual break in play during the fourth Test at Manchester, when Warwick Armstrong disputed an attempt by the England captain to make a declaration not allowed for in the tour regulations. When play resumed after 25 minutes, Armstrong inadvertently bowled a second consecutive over, one on either side of the break.

202 Andy Sandham made his Test debut in the final match at The Oval – the 30th player used by England in the five Tests, a record number in a Test series. Phil Mead scored 182* with a hundred runs coming in the first session on the second day. For the first time in Test cricket, only four bowlers were used in a total that exceeded 400 runs. In England's first-innings total of eight declared for 403, the only Australians to bowl were Jack Gregory (38-5-128-1), Ted McDonald (47-9-143-5), Arthur Mailey (30-4-85-1) and Warwick Armstrong (12-2-44-0).

203 Arthur Mailey took 10 for 66 in Gloucestershire's second innings at Cheltenham, becoming only the second Australian tourist to take all 10 in a first-class match in England.

204 Throughout the five-match Test series, Australia scored its runs at 56.51 per 100 balls faced. England's runs came at a rate of 50.19.

THE TOURISTS

W.W. Armstrong (c), T.J.E. Andrews, W. Bardsley,
H. Carter, H.L. Collins, J.M. Gregory, H.S.T.L. Hendry,
C.G. Macartney, E.A. McDonald, A.A. Mailey, R.E. Mayne,
W.A.S. Oldfield, C.E. Pellew, J. Ryder, J.M. Taylor.

THE RESULTS

TEST MATCHES	FIRST-CLASS MATCHES	ALL MATCHES
P W L D	P W L D	P W L D
5 3 0 2	34 21 2 11	39 23 2 14

1st Test Nottingham: Australia won by 10 wickets
2nd Test Lord's: Australia won by 8 wickets
3rd Test Leeds: Australia won by 219 runs
4th Test Manchester: Drawn
5th Test The Oval: Drawn

1922-23
TOUR OF AUSTRALIA

205 An England team led by Archie MacLaren played seven first-class matches in Australia in 1922-23, either side of a trip to New Zealand. In the MCC's second match against Victoria, the home-side made 6 declared for 617, an innings that included four centuries – 192 by 'Hammy' Love, 101 from Roy Park, 118* by Vernon Ransford and 102 from Arthur Liddicut. The MCC openers batted throughout the final day, with Geoff Wilson (142*) scoring the only hundred of his first-class career. In the second of two appearances by the MCC at the Adelaide Oval, South Australia's Arthur Richardson scored a career-best 280, reaching 100 before lunch on the opening day.

THE TOURISTS

A.C. MacLaren (c), D.F. Brand, F.S.G. Calthorpe,
A.P.F. Chapman, A.P. Freeman, C.H. Gibson, J.C. Hartley,
W.W. Hill-Wood, T.C. Lowry, J.F. MacLean, H.D. Swan,
C.H. Titchmarsh, H. Tyldesley, W.A.C. Wilkinson,
G. Wilson.

THE RESULTS

FIRST-CLASS MATCHES				ALL MATCHES			
P	W	L	D	P	W	L	D
7	0	3	4	8	0	3	5

1924-25
TOUR OF AUSTRALIA

206 South Australia's Vic Richardson became the first captain to lose a first-class match in Australia after making a declaration. Opposing the MCC at the Adelaide Oval, South Australia's first innings was closed at 4 wickets for 346, with an unbeaten double-century (200*) by opening batsman Arthur Richardson – his second score of 200 in consecutive innings for South Australia against the MCC. In reply, the Englishmen made 406, dismissed the home-side for 103, and lost a single wicket in their pursuit of an eventual nine-wicket victory.

207 All eleven England players bowled in the second innings of the match against an Australian XI at the Exhibition Ground in Brisbane. It gave England's wicket-keeper Bert Strudwick a rare opportunity at the bowling crease and he took the only wicket of his first-class career. He had Ron Oxenham stumped by substitute wicket-keeper 'Tich' Freeman, who had dismissed the same batsman, stumped by Strudwick, in the first innings – a unique occurrence in Australian first-class cricket.

208 The first Test at Sydney was highlighted by two century opening partnerships (157 & 110) by its new pair at the top of the order Jacks Hobbs and Herbert Sutcliffe, both of whom made identical innings of 115 in the match. Bill Ponsford (110) became the third

Australian batsman to score a century on his Test debut. Johnny Taylor (108) scored his only Test century and shared an Australian record tenth-wicket partnership of 127 with Arthur Mailey (46*). This was the first Test match in which eight-ball overs were used.

209 Australia became the first country to score 600 in a Test innings in the second match at Melbourne. Bill Ponsford, with 128, became the first batsman to score centuries in his first two Tests. Jack Hobbs and Herbert Sutcliffe opened the England innings with 283, their third consecutive century partnership, and became the first pair to bat undefeated throughout an entire day in a Test match and in a first-class match in Australia. Sutcliffe, with innings of 176 and 127, was the first batsman to score a century in each innings of a Test match against Australia, and the first to score three successive Test hundreds, following his 115 at Sydney. This was the first cricket match in the world with a combined spectator attendance in excess of 200,000.

210 The third Test match at Adelaide lasted seven days, as had the previous two. Jack Ryder scored an unbeaten 201, equalling the highest score to date by an Australian batsman against England.

211 After scoring a duck in the MCC innings of 500 against Victoria, Johnny Douglas was involved in a serious car accident and took no further part in the match, or the tour.

212 With an innings of 143 in the fourth Test at Melbourne, Herbert Sutcliffe became the first batsman to score four centuries in a Test series, reaching the milestone of 1000 Test runs in a record nine matches and 12 innings. This was his third hundred in successive Test innings at the MCG, and for the third time in this series he batted throughout a day's play. Australia's Bert Oldfield became the first wicket-keeper to achieve five dismissals – and four stumpings – in a Test innings. England won the match by an innings and 29 runs, their first Test victory over Australia since 1912.

213 The match between New South Wales and the MCC at Sydney was the first in Australia in which both teams scored 600 runs in an innings. Three batsmen scored centuries in the MCC's 626, which was followed by 619 from NSW, an innings dominated by Herbie Collins' 173 and Tommy Andrews' 224.

214 Clarrie Grimmett became the first Australian bowler to take 10 wickets on his Test debut with five wickets in each innings of the fifth Test at Melbourne. Jack Hobbs and Herbert Sutcliffe both made ducks, one in either innings, the latter ending the series with a then-record 734 runs at 81.55. Maurice Tate completed the rubber with 38 wickets, a record series aggregate by an England bowler in Australia. His haul of 77 first-class wickets remains the record for an England tourist in Australia. He took five wickets in an innings seven times and twice claimed 10 wickets in a match. Arthur Richardson completed the Test series with an identical average of 31.00 for both bat and ball.

THE TOURISTS

A.E.R. Gilligan (c), J.L. Bryan, A.P.F. Chapman,
J.W.H.T. Douglas, A.P. Freeman, J.W. Hearne,
E.H. Hendren, J.B. Hobbs, H. Howell, R. Kilner,
A. Sandham, H. Strudwick, H. Sutcliffe, M.W. Tate,
R.K. Tyldesley, W.W. Whysall, F.E. Woolley.

THE RESULTS

TEST MATCHES	FIRST-CLASS MATCHES	ALL MATCHES
P W L D	P W L D	P W L D
5 1 4 0	17 7 6 4	23 8 6 9

1st Test Sydney: Australia won by 193 runs
2nd Test Melbourne: Australia won by 81 runs
3rd Test Adelaide: Australia won by 11 runs
4th Test Melbourne: England won by innings and 29 runs
5th Test Sydney: Australia won by 307 runs

1926
TOUR OF ENGLAND

215 Bill Woodfull began the 1926 tour in fine style, becoming the second Australian batsman to score a double-century on his first-class debut in England. His 201 against Essex at Leyton was followed by 118 against Surrey at The Oval, an innings that contained just one boundary.

AUSTRALIA VERSUS ENGLAND 1861-2005

216 Warren Bardsley scored an unbeaten 193 opening the batting in the second Test at Lord's. Aged 43 years and 201 days, he is the oldest Australian batsman to score a Test century against England. Jack Hobbs scored 119, during which he became the first batsman to reach 4000 Test runs. Charles Macartney (133*) and 'Patsy' Hendren (127*) also scored hundreds in this match and, at 37 years of age, Hendren was the youngest of the four. This was the first Test match for Harold Larwood, who began his England career with a modest return of three wickets.

217 Warren Bardsley followed his unbeaten century at Lord's with a first-ball duck in the third Test at Leeds. Charles Macartney (151) scored a century before lunch on the opening day and shared a then-record second-wicket partnership of 235 with Bill Woodfull (141). Jack Hobbs became the leading run-scorer in Ashes Tests, overtaking Clem Hill's aggregate of 2660 runs.

218 In the fourth match at Manchester, the 40-year-old Charles Macartney (109) scored his third century in successive Test innings, becoming the first batsman to score three hundreds in a Test series in England.

219 The final Test at The Oval was highlighted by the absence of Frank Woolley, ending a sequence of 52 Tests, and the recall of Wilfred Rhodes, at the age of 48. Jacks Hobbs and Herbert Sutcliffe shared an opening partnership of 172, with England winning by 289 runs and regaining the Ashes.

THE TOURISTS

H.L. Collins (c), T.J.E. Andrews, W. Bardsley, J.L. Ellis,
S.C. Everett, J.M. Gregory, C.V. Grimmett,
H.S.T.L. Hendry, C.G. Macartney, A.A. Mailey,
W.A.S. Oldfield, W.H. Ponsford, A.J. Richardson, J. Ryder,
J.M. Taylor, W.M. Woodfull.

THE RESULTS

TEST MATCHES				FIRST-CLASS MATCHES				ALL MATCHES			
P	W	L	D	P	W	L	D	P	W	L	D
5	0	1	4	33	9	12	3	40	12	1	27

1st Test Nottingham: Drawn
2nd Test Lord's: Drawn
3rd Test Leeds: Drawn
4th Test Manchester: Drawn
5th Test The Oval: England won by 289 runs

1928-29
Tour of Australia

220 Suffering severe rheumatism, Nottinghamshire fast bowler Sam Staples was forced to return home without playing in a single match.

221 The MCC made its highest total in first-class cricket in Australia in 1928-29, with 7 declared for 734 against New South Wales at the SCG. Walter Hammond top-scored with 225 and followed it by taking a wicket with his first ball. Don Bradman scored a century (132*) in his first match against a touring team, and shared a match-saving fourth-wicket partnership of 249 with Alan Kippax (136*).

222 The first Test match of the series, played at a new venue – the Gabba in Brisbane – saw England record the biggest victory by a runs margin in Test history. England's Percy Chapman made the first declaration in a Test match in Australia, closing the second innings at 8 down for 342 and setting Australia an impossible target of 742 for victory. Bill Woodfull carried his bat for 30 in a total of 66, Australia losing by 675 runs. Harold Larwood, in his first Test in Australia, recorded the match-double of eight wickets and 100 runs (70 & 37), while Don Bradman on his debut, scored 18 and one. The other Australian to make his first international appearance in this match was the Victorian left-arm medium-pacer 'Dainty' Ironmonger, who, at the age of 46 years 237 days, was the oldest Australian to make his Test debut – a record he would hold for just two weeks.

223 Following his double-failure with the bat at Brisbane, Don Bradman was dropped for the second Test at Sydney, but fielded throughout both innings after Bill Ponsford had fractured his left hand. All eleven England batsmen reached double figures in its first-innings total of 636, that included a maiden Test-match double-century by Walter Hammond (251). Jack Ryder (79) reached 50 in the second innings in 36 minutes, equalling the fastest 50 on record by an Australian batsman against England. At the age of 46 years 253 days, Don Blackie became Australia's oldest Test debutant.

224 In the third Test at Melbourne, Walter Hammond (200) became the first batsman to score double-centuries in consecutive Test innings. Five other batsmen scored centuries, including the recalled Don Bradman (112).

225 Walter Hammond (119* & 177) continued his impressive form in the fourth Test at Adelaide, becoming the second batsman, after Herbert Sutcliffe, to score four hundreds in a Test series. Archie Jackson, aged 19 years 152 days, scored 164 on his debut, becoming the youngest batsman to score a century in Tests between Australia and England.

226 The fifth Test at Melbourne lasted eight days and remains the longest first-class match in Australia. Following Archie Jackson's hundred at the age of 19 in the previous Test, Jack Hobbs (142) became the oldest batsman to score a Test century (46 years 82 days) and was the first to reach 5000 Test runs during his second-innings knock of 65. Walter Hammond, with innings of 38 and 16, took his series aggregate to 905 runs (average 113.12), a record for an England batsman in Test cricket and remains the Test record for any batsman in Australia. He also became the first England batsman to pass 1500 first-class runs on an Australian tour, scoring a record 1553 runs, average 91.35, in 13 matches.

227 Australia scored nine centuries and England eight in the series, for a total of 17 – a record number in an Ashes rubber.

THE TOURISTS

A.P.F. Chapman (c), L.E.G. Ames, G. Duckworth,
A.P. Freeman, G. Geary, W.R. Hammond, E.H. Hendren,
J.B. Hobbs, D.R. Jardine, H. Larwood, M. Leyland,
C.P. Mead, S.J. Staples, H. Sutcliffe, M.W. Tate,
G.E. Tyldesley, J.C. White.

THE RESULTS

TEST MATCHES					FIRST-CLASS MATCHES					ALL MATCHES			
P	W	L	D		P	W	L	D		P	W	L	D
5	4	1	0		17	8	1	8		24	10	11	3

1st Test Brisbane: England won by 675 runs
2nd Test Sydney: England won by 8 wickets
3rd Test Melbourne: England won by 3 wickets
4th Test Adelaide: England won by 12 runs
5th Test Melbourne: Australia won by 5 wickets

1929-30
Tour of Australia

228 En route to New Zealand for an inaugural Test series, the MCC played five first-class matches in Australia, In the game against Victoria, Bill Woodfull scored a duck and 100*. In the New South Wales match, a total of six batsmen scored centuries, including Arthur Allsopp (117) on his first-class debut. Queensland won its first-ever first-class match against an England side, a feat they would not repeat until 1982-83.

THE TOURISTS

A.H.H. Gilligan (c), M.J.C. Allom, F. Barratt, E.T. Benson,
E.H. Bowley, W. Cornford, E.W. Dawson, K.S. Duleepsinhji,
G.F. Earle, G.B. Legge, M.S. Nichols, M.J.L. Turnbull,
F.E. Woolley, T.S. Worthington.
(Reinforcement: A. Ducat).

THE RESULTS

FIRST-CLASS MATCHES					ALL MATCHES			
P	W	L	D		P	W	L	D
5	2	2	1		5	2	2	1

1930
TOUR OF ENGLAND

229 Don Bradman began his first tour of England by scoring 236 against Worcestershire, the highest debut first-class innings by an Australian batsman in Britain. He also scored a century in his next innings – 185* v Leicestershire at Leicester.

230 Don Bradman (131) scored Australia's first Test century at Nottingham in his first Test in England. The home-side won the first match of the series by 93 runs, the only occasion Australia lost a Test in which D.G. Bradman had scored a century.

231 In the second Test at Lord's, Percy Chapman (121) and Bill Woodfull (155) provided the first occasion in Ashes cricket of opposing captains each scoring centuries in the same match. Don Bradman (254) made the highest innings by an Australian in a Test match at Lord's, forming part of Australia's highest Test total against England – 6 declared for 729. K.S. Duleepsinhji (173) emulated his uncle, K.S. Ranjitsinhji, by scoring a century in his first Test against Australia.

232 The third Test at Leeds was dominated by the 21-year-old Don Bradman, who scored 334, his third century in successive matches. On the first day, Bradman scored a Test-record 309 runs, with 105 in the first session and 115 between lunch and tea. His 200 was reached in 214 minutes, the fastest double-century in Test cricket and, at the time, he was the youngest batsman to reach a Test-match 300. Both Bradman and Walter Hammond reached 1000 runs in Anglo-Australian Tests. Bradman did so in a record 13 innings, Hammond 14.

233 In the final Test at The Oval, Don Bradman (232) scored his third double-century in four matches and increased his aggregate to 974 runs, average 139.14 – a tally that remains the world record for any Test series. This was the final Test match for the 47-year-old Jack Hobbs, who left the scene with the record for most Test runs against Australia – 3636 at 54.26. Australia won the match and regained the Ashes on the 33rd birthday of the captain Bill Woodfull.

234 The 29th tour match, against Gloucestershire at Bristol, resulted in the first tie involving an Australian first-class team. The county side made 72 and 202, the Australians 157 and 117.

235 Of the many records Don Bradman made on his first tour of England, one, in particular, will always remain his. He recorded a 78 rpm disc in London, featuring two piano pieces – 'Old Fashioned Locket' and 'Our Bungalow of Dreams'.

THE TOURISTS

W.M. Woodfull (c), E.L. a'Beckett, D.G. Bradman,
A.G. Fairfax, C.V. Grimmett, P.M. Hornibrook,
A. Hurwood, A. Jackson, A.F. Kippax, S.J. McCabe,
W.A.S. Oldfield, W.H. Ponsford, V.Y. Richardson,
C.W. Walker, T.W. Wall.

THE RESULTS

TEST MATCHES	FIRST-CLASS MATCHES	ALL MATCHES
P W L D	P W L D T	P W L D T
5 2 1 2	31 11 1 18 1	33 12 1 19 1

1st Test Nottingham: England won by 93 runs
2nd Test Lord's: Australia won by 7 wickets
3rd Test Leeds: Drawn
4th Test Manchester: Drawn
5th Test The Oval: Australia won by an innings and 39 runs

1932-33
TOUR OF AUSTRALIA

236 The summer of 1932-33 saw the 24th English team in Australia – one of the most tempestuous and bitter cricket tours of all time. This was the 'Bodyline' series, in which the England captain Douglas Jardine devised a plan of a packed leg-side field and fast short-pitched bowling aimed at the upper bodies of the Australian batsmen. It was principally designed to curb the effectiveness of one Don Bradman.

237 The first signs of bodyline bowling surfaced in the second Australian XI match, at Melbourne, with England's pace-trio of Harold Larwood, Bill Voce and Bill Bowes in operation. Bill Woodfull sustained a blow to the chest, but resumed his innings within a few minutes. The match set a new attendance record in Australian first-class cricket outside Tests, with 109,501 spectators over the four days of play.

238 In the match against New South Wales at Sydney, 'Hammy' Love – not selected in the XI – made three dismissals in the MCC's first innings, keeping for Bert Oldfield, who was laid down with the 'flu. He became the first substitute to make a stumping in Australian first-class cricket, achieving two – a world-first.

239 The first Test match of the series, at Sydney, was dominated by an unbeaten innings of 187 by Stan McCabe, scored against the short-pitched bowling of Bill Voce and Harold Larwood. Herbert Sutcliffe (194) scored his 16th and final Test-match century, while Walter Hammond (112) scored England's 100th Test century in Australia. Nawab of Pataudi Snr, the third Indian prince to represent England, and one who deplored the bodyline tactics of his captain, scored a century (102) in his first Test. Harold Larwood took 10 wickets in the match, England gaining victory by 10 wickets.

240 For the second Test at Melbourne, England went into the match without a slow bowler and suffered defeat. Bill Bowes took his only wicket of the series dismissing Don Bradman first-ball. The Don's first duck against England was coupled with a second-innings century (103*). The leg-spinning Bill O'Reilly took his first ten-wicket haul in a Test, taking five England wickets in each innings.

241 The third Test at Adelaide saw bodyline bowling reach its crescendo, with Bert Oldfield hit on the head, attempting a hook off Harold Larwood, during the first innings. The wicket-keeper suffered a fractured skull and took no further part in the match. Bill Woodfull, who also sustained a painful blow, to the heart, scored 73* in Australia's second-innings 193, becoming the first batsman to carry his bat twice in Test cricket.

242 Six half-centuries, but no hundreds, were scored in the fourth Test at Brisbane. Eddie Paynter, suffering from acute tonsillitis, played two heroic innings. Leaving his sick-bed, he made 83 in the first innings and hit 14* in the second, including a six off Stan McCabe to win the match.

243 Australia began each innings of the final Test at the SCG in the worst possible way. Vic Richardson, who made a pair, and Bill Woodfull recorded Australia's first instance of a 0 & 0 opening partnership in a Test match. Harold Larwood marked his final appearance for England by scoring a career-best 98 batting as a night-watchman. Walter Hammond scored a century (101) in the first innings and 75* in the second, and hit a six to seal the match, England winning cricket's most infamous Test series 4-1. Although Don Bradman failed to score as freely as he had done before, he still managed to top Australia's Test averages, with 396 runs at 56.57.

244 The MCC's penultimate match of the 1932-33 tour, against Victoria in Melbourne, resulted in the first tie in first-class cricket in Australia (Victoria 327 & 3-177, MCC 321 & 9d-183).

245 One of the stumps used in the first Test at Sydney was sold for $2000 at an auction in Adelaide in 1996. The brass-topped stump had been souvenired by 'Tim' Wall, the South Australian fast bowler who topped the Australian bowling averages in the bodyline series, with 16 wickets at 25.56 from four Tests.

THE TOURISTS

D.R. Jardine (c), G.O.B. Allen, L.E.G. Ames, F.R. Brown, W.E. Bowes, G. Duckworth, W.R. Hammond, H. Larwood, M. Leyland, T.B. Mitchell, Nawab of Pataudi Snr, E. Paynter, H. Sutcliffe, M.W. Tate, H. Verity, W. Voce, R.E.S. Wyatt.

THE RESULTS

TEST MATCHES				FIRST-CLASS MATCHES					ALL MATCHES				
P	W	L	D	P	W	L	D	T	P	W	L	D	T
5	4	1	0	17	10	1	5	1	22	10	1	10	1

1st Test Sydney: England won by 10 wickets
2nd Test Melbourne: Australia won by 111 runs
3rd Test Adelaide: England won by 338 runs
4th Test Brisbane: England won by 6 wickets
5th Test Sydney: England won by 8 wickets

1934
Tour of England

246 The first Test match at Trent Bridge saw Australia's Arthur Chipperfield become the first batsman to be dismissed for 99 on his debut. Australia won the match by 238 runs without the bodyline tactics of the previous Ashes series, and without a century from Don Bradman (29 & 25). Ken Farnes marked his England debut with 10 wickets (5-102 & 5-77).

247 England comprehensively outplayed Australia in the following Test, winning by an innings and 38 runs – their first triumph over Australia at Lord's since 1896. Hedley Verity, the Yorkshire left-arm spinner, claimed 14 wickets for 80 on the third day, and finished with a match-haul of 15 for 104 – England's best bowling performance to date against Australia. The two wicket-keepers created history, with England's Les Ames (120) scoring the first century by a keeper in an Ashes Test and Bert Oldfield becoming the first to reach the Test double of 1000 runs and 100 dismissals. In his second Test appearance, Australia's Bill Brown scored a maiden century (105).

248 The third Test at Manchester began with a huge total from England – 6 declared for 627 – including hundreds from the 45-year-old 'Patsy' Hendren (132) and Maurice Leyland (153). Bill O'Reilly took three wickets in four balls, while 'Gubby' Allen began his bowling spell with an uncharacteristic 13-ball over, and finished Australia's first innings with none for 113. For the first time in Ashes history, one team recorded a difference of over 500 runs between innings totals – 504 by England (9d-627 & 0d-123).

249 Don Bradman scored his second triple-century in successive Test appearances at Leeds, scoring 304 and sharing an Australian record fourth-wicket partnership of 388 with Bill Ponsford (181).

250 In the fifth Test at The Oval, Don Bradman (244) and Bill Ponsford (266) recorded their second triple-century stand in successive innings, posting 451 for the second wicket – the highest partnership by Australia in Test-match cricket. Frank Woolley, back in the England XI at the age of 47, deputised for Les Ames in the second innings and conceded 37 byes, a record number in Tests. Australia (701 & 327) beat

England (321 & 145) by 562 runs, their biggest victory by a runs-margin in Test cricket.

251 In a match against an England XI at Folkestone, Don Bradman became the first batsman in first-class cricket to score 30 runs off a single six-ball over. In successive balls from spinner 'Tich' Freeman, Bradman hit 4, 6, 6, 4, 6 and 4.

252 For the first time in English first-class cricket, the seasonal batting and bowling averages were topped by Australian tourists – Don Bradman: 2020 runs at 84.16 and Bill O'Reilly: 109 wickets at 17.04.

THE TOURISTS

W.M. Woodfull (c), B.A. Barnett, D.G. Bradman,
E.H. Bromley, W.A. Brown, A.G. Chipperfield, L.S. Darling,
H.I. Ebeling, L.O. Fleetwood-Smith, C.V. Grimmett,
A.F. Kippax, S.J. McCabe, W.A.S. Oldfield, W.J. O'Reilly,
W.H. Ponsford, T.W. Wall.

THE RESULTS

TEST MATCHES	FIRST-CLASS MATCHES	ALL MATCHES
P W L D	P W L D	P W L D
5 2 1 2	30 13 1 16	34 15 11 8

1st Test Nottingham: Australia won by 238 runs
2nd Test Lord's: England won by an innings and 38 runs
3rd Test Manchester: Drawn
4th Test Leeds: Drawn
5th Test The Oval: Australia won by 562 runs

1935-36
TOUR OF AUSTRALIA

253 England played a six-match tour of Australia in 1935-36 en route to New Zealand. In the first match, against Western

Australia at the WACA, Norman Mitchell-Innes hit 30 in 13 minutes in the second innings. His first scoring strokes were 4, 4, 4, 6 and 6. In the next match, at the Adelaide Oval, Don Bradman scored a half-century on his first-class debut for South Australia and Mervyn Waite performed the hat-trick to end the MCC's first innings. England's only loss came at the SCG, where New South Wales, captained by the future ABC cricket commentator Alan McGilvray, gained victory by 10 wickets.

THE TOURISTS

E.R.T. Holmes (c), W. Barber, A.D. Baxter, S.C. Griffith,
J. Hardstaff Jnr, J.H. Human, J. Langridge, C.J. Lyttelton,
N.S. Mitchell-Innes, J.H. Parks, A.G. Powell, H.D. Read,
J.M. Sims, D. Smith.

THE RESULTS

FIRST-CLASS MATCHES	ALL MATCHES
P W L D	P W L D
6 3 1 2	6 3 1 2

1936-37
TOUR OF AUSTRALIA

254 With twin-knocks of 104 & 136 in the match against South Australia, Walter Hammond became the first English tourist to score centuries in four successive innings in Australian first-class cricket, after 141 against Western Australia at Perth and 107 against a Combined XI at Perth.

255 Bill Brown (74) and Rex Rogers (62) recorded Queensland's first century opening partnership against an England team in the match at the Gabba. The MCC replied with a 295-run opening stand from Arthur Fagg (112) and Charlie Barnett (259), the highest to date for the first wicket in a first-class match in Brisbane.

256 In the first Test at Brisbane, England opener Stan Worthington was out to the first ball of the match in his first Test against Australia. Jack Fingleton scored 100 in the first innings and was out first-ball in the second. 'Jack' Badcock, on his Test debut, also made a duck in the second innings, as did Don Bradman in his first Test as Australian captain. 'Gubby' Allen, with 35 and 68 and 3 for 71 and 5 for 36, became the first captain in Ashes cricket to score 100 runs and take eight wickets in a match.

257 Don Bradman made his second duck in successive Test innings, out first-ball to Bill Voce in the second Test at Sydney. Walter Hammond, who made a duck in the first Test, scored 231*, his fourth hundred in four Tests at the SCG.

258 Over 350,000 people attended the rain-affected third Test at Melbourne, a record crowd for a first-class match in Australia. For the first time in Test cricket, both sides declared their first innings closed. Stan Worthington, in his second Test of the series, was out for his second duck, to the third ball of England's first innings. Facing a 'sticky' wicket, Australia's second innings was opened by tail-enders Bill O'Reilly and 'Chuck' Fleetwood-Smith, a move designed to allow the more-recognised batsmen to take advantage of improved conditions. Jack Fingleton (136) and Don Bradman (270) added 346 runs, the record sixth-wicket partnership in Test cricket, with the captain's contribution being the highest second-innings score in Australia-England Tests and the highest by a No.7 batsman in a Test. Bradman also became the first batsman to reach 1000 runs during the course of five consecutive Tests (304, 244 & 77 v England in 1934 and 38, 0, 0, 82, 13 & 270 in 1936-37).

259 In the fourth Test at Adelaide, Don Bradman, for the third time, scored a double-century in two consecutive Tests against England. During his knock of 212, he became Australia's highest first-class run-scorer, beating Clem Hill's record of 11,137.

260 Australia secured its third consecutive victory of the rubber at Melbourne – the first time a country had won a Test series after losing the first two matches. Don Bradman scored 169 out of 604 and took his series aggregate to 810 runs, a new record for a captain in a Test series. The five Test matches attracted a crowd estimated to be around 950,000 – a record for any Test series.

THE TOURISTS

G.O.B. Allen (c), L.E.G. Ames, C.J. Barnett, W.H. Copson,
G. Duckworth, A.E. Fagg, K. Farnes, L.B. Fishlock,
W.R. Hammond, J. Hardstaff Jnr, M. Leyland,
R.W.V. Robins, J.M. Sims, H. Verity, W. Voce,
T.S. Worthington, R.E.S. Wyatt.
(Reinforcement: T.H. Wade).

THE RESULTS

TEST MATCHES				FIRST-CLASS MATCHES				ALL MATCHES			
P	W	L	D	P	W	L	D	P	W	L	D
5	2	3	0	17	5	5	7	24	7	5	12

1st Test Brisbane: England won by 322 runs
2nd Test Sydney: England won by an innings and 22 runs
3rd Test Melbourne: Australia won by 365 runs
4th Test Adelaide: Australia won by 148 runs
5th Test Melbourne: Australia won by an innings and 200 runs

1938
TOUR OF ENGLAND

261 The 19th Australian team to play in England began its campaign with five consecutive first-class totals of over 500 – 541 v Worcestershire at Worcester, 7 declared for 679 v Oxford University at Oxford, 5 declared for 590 v Leicestershire at Leicester, 5 declared for 708 v Cambridge University at Cambridge and 502 v MCC at Lord's. After making 6 declared for 406 in their next first-class match, against Northamptonshire, the Australians once again topped the 500-mark, with 528 against Surrey at The Oval.

262 Don Bradman (258) began the tour with his customary double-century against Worcestershire, after 206 in 1934 and 236 in 1930. On his first-class debut in England, Victorian bowler Ernie

McCormick was no-balled 35 times for over-stepping the crease in the match at Worcester. His first over lasted 14 balls, his second 15.

263 The first Test at Nottingham saw the scoring of four hundreds in England's first innings and seven for the match – both remain records in Ashes Tests. Len Hutton (100) and Denis Compton (102) both reached three-figures in their first Test against Australia. At 20 years 19 days, Compton became the youngest England batsman to score a Test hundred. Don Bradman (144*) scored a record-13th century against England.

264 Walter Hammond scored 240 in the second Test, the highest innings by an England captain against Australia and the highest score against Australia at Lord's. Bill Brown replied with a double-century in Australia's first innings, carrying his bat for 206*. It was the 100th century by an Australian against England, while the 102* scored by Don Bradman was the 200th century in Australia-England Tests.

265 Don Bradman, with 103, scored his third century in successive Test innings at Headingley. Australia retained the Ashes during the fourth Test, in which Bill O'Reilly took 10 wickets.

266 The final Test match at The Oval saw England record the highest total in Test cricket to date and the biggest victory margin. Len Hutton made 364, England's highest individual Test score, which spanned 13 hours and 17 minutes – the longest innings against Australia. His triple-century was England's 100th hundred against Australia and, with Maurice Leyland (187), Hutton shared a second-wicket stand of 382 – England's record partnership for that wicket against all countries. Leyland also became the first batsman to score centuries in his first and last Test innings against Australia. 'Chuck' Fleetwood-Smith conceded a record 298 runs in England's 7 declared for 903, scored off 335.2 overs. Australia was without two of its key batsmen – Don Bradman and Jack Fingleton – who were absent injured, and was never in the hunt. The Australians made 201 and 123, going down by an innings and 579 runs.

267 Don Bradman set a new record for the highest average in a first-class season in England, becoming the first batsman to exceed 100. From 26 first-class innings, Bradman scored 2429 runs at 115.66.

AUSTRALIA VERSUS ENGLAND 1861-2005

THE TOURISTS

D.G. Bradman (c), C.L. Badcock, S.G. Barnes,
B.A. Barnett, W.A. Brown, A.G. Chipperfield,
J.H.W. Fingleton, L.O. Fleetwood-Smith, A.L. Hassett,
S.J. McCabe, E.L. McCormick, W.J. O'Reilly, M.G. Waite,
C.W. Walker, F.A. Ward, E.C.S. White.

THE RESULTS

TEST MATCHES	FIRST-CLASS MATCHES	ALL MATCHES
P W L D	P W L D	P W L D
4 1 1 2	29 15 2 12	35 20 2 13

1st Test Nottingham: Drawn
2nd Test Lord's: Drawn
3rd Test Manchester: Abandoned
4th Test Leeds: Australia won by 5 wickets
5th Test The Oval: England won by an innings and 579 runs

1945-1968

1945
TOUR OF ENGLAND

268 International cricket resumed in England after the Second World War with a series of matches organised by the RAAF and the AIF. A 17-man team captained by Lindsay Hassett undertook a goodwill tour of England playing five first-class matches known as the 'Victory Tests'. The leading batsman on tour was Keith Miller, who scored a century (105) on his first-class debut in England, and finished with 514 runs, in six matches, at an average of 64.25. In the five 'Test' matches, he hit 443 runs and took 10 wickets.

THE TOURISTS

A.L. Hassett (c), C.D. Bremner, D.K. Carmody,
A.G. Cheetham, D.R. Cristofani, R.S. Ellis, K.R. Miller,
C.G. Pepper, J. Pettiford, C.F.T. Price, A.W. Roper,
S.G. Sismey, R.M. Stanford, R.S. Whitington, E.A. Williams,
R.G. Williams, J.A. Workman.

THE RESULTS

TEST MATCHES	FIRST-CLASS MATCHES	ALL MATCHES
P W L D	P W L D	P W L D
– – – –	6 3 2 1	20 7 6 7

1946-47
TOUR OF AUSTRALIA

269 The battle against England resumed following an eight-year break with a record margin of victory in Australia in the first Test at Brisbane. Don Bradman (187) and vice-captain Lindsay Hassett (128) added a record 276 for the third wicket. In his second Test match, and his first against England, Colin McCool (95) failed by five runs in reaching a maiden Test century. Following a violent hailstorm, 15 England wickets fell in a little under four hours, with Australia wrapping-up the opening Test in decisive fashion, winning by an innings and 332 runs.

270 Don Bradman and Sid Barnes both hit 234 in Australia's only innings in the second Test, and in partnership scored 405 for the fifth wicket, the highest for that wicket in all Tests. Godfrey Evans did not concede a bye during Australia's total of 8 declared for 659 and his effort remains a Test wicket-keeping record. Victorian pace bowler Fred Freer marked his only Test-match appearance by taking a wicket in his first over, a feat emulated later in the match by Ian Johnson.

271 Following two innings victories for the Australians, the third Test at Melbourne produced the first drawn result in Australia since 1881-82. Colin McCool made up for his 95 at Brisbane by posting his sole Test century (104*). In the second innings Ray Lindwall, batting at No.9, also brought up a maiden Test hundred (100) and scored a whirlwind 154 runs in 88 minutes with Don Tallon (92).

272 In the fourth Test at Adelaide, England's Denis Compton (147 & 103*) and Australia's Arthur Morris (122 & 124*) made history by both scoring two centuries, the first occasion a batsman from each side had performed the feat in the same Test. Godfrey Evans took 97 minutes (and 61 balls) to score his first run in the second innings, a record in all first-class cricket.

273 Don Bradman, with 680 runs in the five matches, became the first batsman to score 500 runs in consecutive Test series in Australia. In the 1936-37 series against England Bradman had scored 810 runs, average 90.00.

THE TOURISTS

W.R. Hammond (c), A.V. Bedser, D.C.S. Compton,
W.J. Edrich, T.G. Evans, L.B. Fishlock, P.A. Gibb,
J. Hardstaff Jnr, L. Hutton, J.T. Ikin, J. Langridge,
R. Pollard, T.P.B. Smith, W. Voce, C. Washbrook,
D.V.P. Wright, N.W.D. Yardley.

THE RESULTS

TEST MATCHES				FIRST-CLASS MATCHES				ALL MATCHES			
P	W	L	D	P	W	L	D	P	W	L	D
5	0	3	2	17	1	3	13	25	4	3	18

1st Test Brisbane: Australia won by an innings and 332 runs
2nd Test Sydney: Australia won by an innings and 33 runs
3rd Test Melbourne: Drawn
4th Test Adelaide: Drawn
5th Test Sydney: Australia won by 5 wickets

1948
TOUR OF ENGLAND

274 Don Bradman began his final tour of England as he began his first, in 1930, by scoring a century – for the fourth time – in the opening first-class match against Worcestershire.

275 The Australians made a whopping 721 on the opening day of the match against Essex at Southend, the most runs scored by one team in a day in first-class cricket. Don Bradman made 187, Bill Brown 153, Sam Loxton 120 and Ron Saggers 104*. Keith Miller was out for a duck!

276 In the opening Test match at Nottingham, Don Bradman (138) scored his 28th Test century, while both Lindsay Hassett (137) and Denis Compton (184) made their highest scores in Ashes cricket.

277 For Don Bradman, the second match at Lord's was the 14th consecutive Ashes Test in which he batted that he scored a half-century. His second-innings knock was brought to a close on 89 by Alec Bedser who had claimed his wicket in all four innings of the series so far. This was the 150th Test match between Australia and England.

278 Denis Compton scored a century (145) and a duck in the third Test at Old Trafford, following on from Don Bradman (138 & 0) in the first Test and Sid Barnes (0 & 141) in the second. Gloucestershire batsman George Emmett scored 10 and 0 in his only Test appearance for England, brought in at the expense of Len Hutton who was dropped.

279 Australia achieved a remarkable victory in the fourth Test at Leeds after being set 404 in 344 minutes on a spinning wicket.

With centuries from Arthur Morris and Don Bradman, Australia became the first country to score 400 in the fourth innings and win. Bradman's 173* was his last century in Test cricket and his 19th against England. Sam Loxton hit five sixes during his innings of 93, while the 19-year-old Neil Harvey (112) became the first Australian left-handed batsman to score a century in his debut Test against England. 1723 runs were scored with the loss of 31 wickets – the first time an aggregate of 1700 runs had been recorded in a first-class match in England.

280 In his final Test match for Australia, at The Oval, Don Bradman, requiring just four runs for a career-average of 100, was dismissed for a duck by Eric Hollies. After 37 Test matches against England Bradman left the scene with the most runs (5028), most centuries (19), most double-centuries (8) and most triple-centuries (2). England was dismissed for 52, its lowest total against Australia last century, and lost by an innings and 149 runs.

281 Don Bradman concluded his illustrious first-class career in England by scoring centuries in his last three innings on tour – 150 v Gentlemen of England at Lord's, 143 v South of England at Hastings and 153 v H.D.G. Leveson-Gower's XI at Scarborough. On each of his four tours to England, Bradman uniquely averaged over 80 – 98.66 in 1930, 84.16 in 1934, 115.66 in 1938 and 89.92 in 1948.

282 The 20th Australian team to play in England remained undefeated in its 31 first-class matches on tour. This had been Australia's greatest triumph. As many as seven batsmen scored 1000 first-class runs, seven averaged over 50 and seven took 50 or more first-class wickets. The best with the ball was Bill Johnston – 102 wickets, average 16.42 – who remains the last Australian bowler to have taken 100 first-class wickets on a tour of England.

THE TOURISTS

D.G. Bradman (c), S.G. Barnes, W.A. Brown, R.A. Hamence,
R.N. Harvey, A.L. Hassett, I.W. Johnson, W.A. Johnston,
R.R. Lindwall, S.J.E. Loxton, C.L. McCool, K.R. Miller,
A.R. Morris, D.T. Ring, R.A. Saggers, D. Tallon,
E.R.H. Toshack.

THE RESULTS

TEST MATCHES	FIRST-CLASS MATCHES	ALL MATCHES
P W L D	P W L D	P W L D
5 4 0 1	31 23 0 8	34 25 0 9

1st Test Nottingham: Australia won by 8 wickets
2nd Test Lord's: Australia won by 409 runs
3rd Test Manchester: Drawn
4th Test Leeds: Australia won by 7 wickets
5th Test The Oval: Australia won by an innings and 149 runs

1950-51
TOUR OF AUSTRALIA

283 On a 'sticky' wicket at Brisbane, the first Test match of the '50-51 series saw both captains make a declaration with the score under 100. England's first innings closed at 7 for 68, 160 runs behind. Twenty wickets tumbled on the third afternoon, with Australia losing its first three batsmen without a run on the board. The declaration came at 7 for 32 and Australia dismissed England for 122, winning an extraordinary match by 70 runs. Jack Moroney, in his only Test against England, opened the Australian innings and made a pair. The 'mystery bowler' Jack Iverson, on his Test debut, was the hero taking 4 for 43.

284 On his Test debut in the third match at Sydney, Middlesex fast bowler John Warr failed to take a wicket and conceded 142 runs in 36 overs. He completed his two-match career in the fourth Test at Adelaide capturing his only Test wicket, that of Ian Johnson, and finished with a Test bowling average of 281.00. The Adelaide Oval Test saw Arthur Morris (206) score the then-highest innings by an Australian left-hander against England, Len Hutton (156*) become the first England batsman to twice carry his bat through a Test innings and Jim Burke (101*) make a century on his debut.

285 England won the fifth Test at Melbourne by a margin of eight wickets, their first victory over Australia since its record performance at The Oval in 1938. England's Reg Simpson made his only Test century (156*) against Australia on his 31st birthday. At the age of 40 years 72 days, Freddie Brown (5-49), became the oldest England bowler to take five wickets in an innings against Australia.

THE TOURISTS

F.R. Brown (c), T.E. Bailey, A.V. Bedser, R. Berry,
D.B. Close, D.C.S. Compton, J.G. Dewes, T.G. Evans,
W.E. Hollies, L. Hutton, A.J.W. McIntyre,
W.G.A. Parkhouse, D.S. Sheppard, R.T. Simpson, J.J. Warr,
C. Washbrook, D.V.P. Wright.
(Reinforcements: E.A. Bedser, J.B. Statham, R. Tattersall).

THE RESULTS

TEST MATCHES	FIRST-CLASS MATCHES	ALL MATCHES
P W L D	P W L D	P W L D
5 1 4 0	16 5 4 7	25 7 4 14

1st Test Brisbane: Australia won by 70 runs
2nd Test Melbourne: Australia won by 28 runs
3rd Test Sydney: Australia won by an innings and 13 runs
4th Test Adelaide: Australia won by 274 runs
5th Test Melbourne: England won by 8 wickets

1953
TOUR OF ENGLAND

286 Three batsmen scored hundreds in the opening first-class match of the tour, against Worcestershire. In the Australians' 7 declared for 542, Keith Miller made 220*, while Graeme Hole and Ron Archer – both on their first-class debuts in England – scored 112 and 108 respectively.

287 After reaching 4 for 237 in the first Test at Nottingham, Australia lost its last seven wickets for just 12 runs, with six batsmen in all falling for a duck. Alec Bedser, with 7 for 55 and then 7 for 44, finished the match with 14 for 99, a record performance in a Test match at Nottingham.

288 Freddie Brown, who, at the time, was England's Chairman of Selectors, came out of retirement for his first Test in two years, at Lord's. Alec Bedser took his third successive haul of five wickets in an innings, during which he became the first England bowler to take 200 Test wickets. Len Hutton made 145 – his fifth and final century against Australia. Willie Watson (109), in his first Test against Australia, and Trevor Bailey (71) saved England from defeat on the final afternoon, adding a priceless 163 runs for the fifth wicket.

289 The third Test at Manchester was ruined by rain, with a little under 14 hours of playing time. Yorkshire spinner Johnny Wardle almost destroyed Australia on his own in the second innings, taking 4 for 7 in five overs. The match ended with Australia at 8 for 35, with Lindsay Hassett and Jim de Courcy the equal top-scorers with eight runs apiece.

290 After four drawn Tests, England won the final Test at The Oval and took the Ashes from Australia after a record period of 18 years and 362 days. Len Hutton became the first captain to win a Test series after losing all five tosses. Alec Bedser, who, during the series had become Test cricket's highest wicket-taker, claimed 39 wickets, then the record for England v Australia.

291 During the final first-class match of the tour, a friendly against T.N. Pearce's XI at Scarborough, Richie Benaud blasted 11 sixes in his knock of 135, becoming the first Australian batsman to score eight sixes in a first-class innings. With a further four boundaries during his innings, Benaud became the first Australian to score a first-class century containing more sixes than fours.

292 Australia's Bill Johnston, a fast bowler, topped England's first-class batting averages in 1953 with 102.00. He was not-out 16 times in 17 innings, scoring 102 runs.

THE TOURISTS

A.L. Hassett (c), R.G. Archer, R. Benaud, I.D. Craig,
A.K. Davidson, J.H. de Courcy, R.N. Harvey, J.C. Hill,
G.B. Hole, W.A. Johnston, G.R.A. Langley, R.R. Lindwall,
C.C. McDonald, K.R. Miller, A.R. Morris, D.T. Ring,
D. Tallon.

THE RESULTS

TEST MATCHES	FIRST-CLASS MATCHES	ALL MATCHES
P W L D	P W L D	P W L D
5 0 1 4	33 16 1 16	35 16 1 18

1st Test Nottingham: Drawn
2nd Test Lord's: Drawn
3rd Test Manchester: Drawn
4th Test Leeds: Drawn
5th Test The Oval: England won by 8 wickets

1954-55
TOUR OF AUSTRALIA

293 For the first time in Australia the pitch for a Test match was completely covered. Len Hutton won the toss in the first Test at Brisbane and sent Australia in to bat. The England captain then sat back and watched Australia pile on a formidable 8 declared for 601. Arthur Morris (153) and Neil Harvey (162) scored what were to be Australia's only two centuries of the five-match series. England went on to lose the opening match by an innings and 154 runs.

294 After being knocked unconscious and losing his wicket, both times, to Ray Lindwall, fast bowler Frank Tyson bowled England to victory in the second Test at Sydney with a match-haul of 10 for 130. Peter May (104) scored his first Test hundred against Australia.

295 In the third Test at Melbourne, Colin Cowdrey became the 50th England batsman to score a Test century against Australia. His runs came in the lowest total in Ashes Tests to contain a century – 102 out of 191 (Don Bradman set the record in the second Test at Melbourne in 1932-33 with 103* in Australia's 191). Frank Tyson once again bowled England to victory, with an inspirational 7 for 27.

296 The tourists won the series with a five-wicket win in the fourth Test at Adelaide, and saw Len Hutton become the first England captain to have won the Ashes and then successfully defend the trophy. For the second Test in a row, England turned superstition to its advantage, by dismissing Australia in its second innings for 111.

297 No play was possible until the afternoon of the fourth day in the final Test at Sydney due to rain. 'Nelson' struck yet again with England's Tom Graveney scoring 111, becoming the 100th player to score a century in Anglo-Australian Tests. Ray Lindwall took his 100th Test wicket against England when Trevor Bailey allowed himself to be bowled, for 72.

THE TOURISTS

L. Hutton (c), K.V. Andrew, R. Appleyard, T.E. Bailey,
A.V. Bedser, D.C.S. Compton, M.C. Cowdrey, W. J. Edrich,
T.G. Evans, T.W. Graveney, P.J. Loader, J.E. McConnon,
P.B.H. May, R.T. Simpson, J.B. Statham, F.H. Tyson,
J.H. Wardle, J.V. Wilson.

THE RESULTS

TEST MATCHES	FIRST-CLASS MATCHES	ALL MATCHES
P W L D	P W L D	P W L D
5 3 1 1	17 8 2 7	23 13 2 8

1st Test Brisbane: Australia won by an innings and 154 runs
2nd Test Sydney: England won by 38 runs
3rd Test Melbourne: England won by 128 runs
4th Test Adelaide: England won by 5 wickets
5th Test Sydney: Drawn

1956
TOUR OF ENGLAND

298 After four consecutive drawn matches against county sides, the Australians lost its first first-class match of the tour at The Oval. Surrey won the match by 10 wickets, after off-spinner Jim Laker had taken 10 for 88 in Australia's first innings of 259.

299 Peter Richardson marked his England debut in the first Test at Trent Bridge by opening the innings with a pair of half-centuries (81 & 73). He became the first batsman to score a 50 in each innings of his first Ashes Test match and not score a century.

300 Australia's first Test victory in England since 1948 came at Lord's, with the 36-year-old Keith Miller (5-72 & 5-80) producing the only ten-wicket haul of his Test career. Australia's Gil Langley became the first wicket-keeper to achieve nine dismissals in a Test, with eight catches and one stumping. Richie Benaud made 97 in the second innings, Australia's highest individual score in the five-match series.

301 England secured its first victory against Australia at Leeds in the third Test which saw the inclusion of England selector Cyril Washbrook, who scored 98, at the age of 41. Peter May (101) – who became the first England batsman to score five consecutive half-centuries against Australia – and Washbrook shared a fourth-wicket partnership of 187.

302 Jim Laker rewrote the record books in the fourth Test at Manchester taking 19 wickets for 90. He became the first bowler to take 18 wickets in a first-class match, the first to take 10 wickets in a Test innings and the first to take 10 wickets in a first-class innings twice in a season. He claimed 9 for 37 in the first innings, including a spell of 7 for 8 in 22 balls, and 10 for 53 in the second – all wickets were taken from the Stretford End. After a first-innings opening stand of 48 between Colin McDonald (32) and Jim Burke (22), Australia lost all of its wickets for 36. Ken 'Slasher' Mackay and Neil Harvey both made pairs, with Harvey twice losing his wicket without scoring on the second day. The world-record performance was recognised by a printing firm, Thomas De La Rue, which presented Laker with £190 – ten pounds for each wicket. With seven wickets in the final Test at The Oval, Laker extended his series-haul to 46 – the most wickets in an Anglo-Australian Test series.

THE TOURISTS

I.W. Johnson (c), R.G. Archer, R. Benaud, P.J.P. Burge,
I.D. Craig, W.P.A. Crawford, A.K. Davidson, R.N. Harvey,
G.R.A. Langley, R.R. Lindwall, C.C. McDonald,
K.D. Mackay, L.V. Maddocks, K.R. Miller, J.W. Rutherford,
J.W. Wilson.

THE RESULTS

TEST MATCHES	FIRST-CLASS MATCHES	ALL MATCHES
P W L D	P W L D	P W L D
5 1 2 2	31 9 3 19	35 12 3 20

1st Test Nottingham: Drawn
2nd Test Lord's: Australia won by 185 runs
3rd Test Leeds: England won by an innings and 42 runs
4th Test Manchester: England won by an innings and 170 runs
5th Test The Oval: Drawn

1958-59
TOUR OF AUSTRALIA

303 The first Test match at Brisbane established several first-class records for slow scoring. In England's second innings Trevor Bailey took 357 minutes to reach 50, the slowest recorded half-century in first-class cricket. His innings of 68 spanned 458 minutes and 425 balls, one of the slowest innings of all time. Jim Burke scored at an even slower pace than Bailey, making 28* in 250 minutes. The fourth day saw the scoring of just 106 runs, the fewest ever scored in a day's Test cricket in Australia. Richie Benaud, who would later became the face of TV-cricket, captained Australia in the first Test series televised in Australia.

304 England began the second Test at Melbourne, losing its first three wickets with just seven runs on the board. Alan Davidson was the destroyer, taking all three of the wickets in his second over, finishing with Test-best figures against England of 6 for 64. England was bundled out 87 in the second innings, its lowest total in Australia since scoring 61 at Melbourne in 1903-04.

305 Colin McDonald (170) became the 50th Australian to score a hundred against England in the fourth Test at Adelaide. He scored another century (133) in his next innings, at Melbourne. Trevor Bailey was out for a pair in this match, in his final Test appearance, to Ray Lindwall, who broke Clarrie Grimmett's Australian Test record of 216 wickets.

THE TOURISTS

P.B.H. May (c), T.E. Bailey, M.C. Cowdrey, T.G. Evans, T.W. Graveney, J.C. Laker, P.J. Loader, G.A.R. Lock, C.A. Milton, P.E. Richardson, J.B. Statham, R. Subba Row, R. Swetman, F.S. Trueman, F.H. Tyson, W. Watson. (Reinforcements: E.R. Dexter, J.B. Mortimore).

THE RESULTS

TEST MATCHES	FIRST-CLASS MATCHES	ALL MATCHES
P W L D	P W L D	P W L D
5 0 4 1	17 4 4 9	20 7 4 9

1st Test Brisbane: Australia won by 8 wickets
2nd Test Melbourne: Australia won by 8 wickets
3rd Test Sydney: Drawn
4th Test Adelaide: Australia won by 10 wickets
5th Test Melbourne: Australia won by 9 wickets

1961
TOUR OF ENGLAND

306 Neil Harvey (114) scored Australia's first Test century at Edgbaston. Four other batsmen passed 50 in Australia's total of 5 declared for 516, including opener Bill Lawry (57) on his Test debut. Raman Subba Row (112) scored a century in his first Test against Australia.

AUSTRALIA VERSUS ENGLAND 1861-2005

307 Bill Lawry (130) scored a century in his first Test appearance at Lord's. Neil Harvey captained Australia for the only time in Test career when he filled in for the injured Richie Benaud, and inflicted upon England its first Test loss in 19 matches.

308 Fred Trueman claimed 11 wickets in the third Test at Leeds, including a spell of 5 for 0 in 24 balls during Australia's second-innings 120. Opening the bowling with 'Fiery Fred' was Derbyshire fast bowler Les Jackson, recalled for his first Test in 12 years.

309 The fourth Test at Manchester saw the marriage of Bill Lawry and Bob Simpson at the top of the order. Their famous association began with a century partnership in the second innings. Earlier in the match, Simpson, bowling leg-spinners, had taken 4 for 2 in 26 balls to end England's first innings. After scoring a duck in the first innings, Alan Davidson made an unbeaten 77 in the second, including 20 runs off one over from David Allen. Richie Benaud took five wickets for 12 in 25 balls in England's second innings, Australia winning the match by 54 runs.

310 Glamorgan's Don Shepherd reached 50 in the match against the Australians at Swansea in just 11 scoring strokes. He got to 51* in 15 minutes, with six sixes, three fours, a two and a one.

311 On his first trip to England, Bill Lawry made 2019 runs, with nine centuries, and remains the last Australian to have scored 2000 first-class runs on an English tour.

THE TOURISTS

R. Benaud (c), B.C. Booth, B.J.P. Burge, A.K. Davidson,
R.A. Gaunt, A.T.W. Grout, R.N. Harvey, B.N. Jarman,
L.F. Kline, W.M. Lawry, C.C. McDonald, K.D. Mackay,
G.D. McKenzie, F.M. Misson, N.C. O'Neill, I.W. Quick,
R.B. Simpson.

THE RESULTS

TEST MATCHES	FIRST-CLASS MATCHES	ALL MATCHES
P W L D	P W L D	P W L D
5 2 1 2	32 13 1 18	37 14 2 21

1st Test Birmingham: Drawn
2nd Test Lord's: Australia won by 5 wickets
3rd Test Leeds: England won by 8 wickets

4th Test Manchester: Australia won by 54 runs
5th Test The Oval: Drawn

1962-63
TOUR OF AUSTRALIA

312 A future federal Defence Minister scored a half-century (53) off the MCC in the first of two matches it played against South Australia in 1962-63. In the MCC's next match, against an Australian XI at Melbourne, Ian McLachlan scored another two half-centuries (55 & 68).

313 Fourteen individual half-centuries were scored in the first Test at Brisbane, with Brian Booth (112) the only batsman to advance to 100.

314 England broke a long drought in Australia winning the second Test at the MCG, its first victory in Australia in eight Tests since 1954-55. Bill Lawry scored a fifty in each innings, the second taking 275 minutes.

315 Bob Simpson recorded his best Test figures in the third Test at Sydney taking 5 for 57. England's wicket-keeper John Murray, batting one-handed due to an injured shoulder, took 100 minutes for his 3* – the slowest innings on record in Australia-England Tests.

316 In the fourth Test at Adelaide, Ken Barrington (132*) became the first England batsman to complete an Ashes century with a six. Neil Harvey (154) scored the last of his 21 Test centuries and his sixth against England.

317 Don Bradman came out of retirement to appear for the Prime Minister's XI against the MCC at Canberra's Manuka Oval. In what turned out to be his last match, Bradman (3) batted with Don Chipp, who later became the leader of the Australian Democrats.

318 England and Australia ended the final match at the SCG with the series squared (1-1), for the first time in a five-match series in Australia. Ken Barrington, with 101 and 94, became the first batsman to score a century and a ninety in the same Ashes Test. Norman O'Neill (73) scored the 1000th half-century in Anglo-Australian Tests, while Alan Davidson, in his final Test, took a wicket with his final ball.

THE TOURISTS

E.R. Dexter (c), D.A. Allen, K.F. Barrington, L.J. Coldwell, M.C. Cowdrey, T.W. Graveney, R. Illingworth, B.R. Knight, J.D.F. Larter, J.T. Murray, P.H. Parfitt, G. Pullar, D.S. Sheppard, A.C. Smith, J.B. Statham, F.J. Titmus, F.S. Trueman.

THE RESULTS

TEST MATCHES	FIRST-CLASS MATCHES	ALL MATCHES
P W L D	P W L D	P W L D
5 1 1 3	15 4 3 8	32 12 3 17

1st Test Brisbane: Drawn
2nd Test Melbourne: England won by 7 wickets
3rd Test Sydney: Australia won by 8 wickets
4th Test Adelaide: Drawn
5th Test Sydney: Drawn

1964
TOUR OF ENGLAND

319 Ian Redpath was no-balled for throwing in the match against Glamorgan at Cardiff. He was called once by umpire J.G. Langridge.

320 When Bob Simpson completed the match against the MCC at Lord's, he had strung together seven fifties in successive first-class innings on the tour to date.

321 The first Test, at Nottingham, saw the England debut of Geoff Boycott, who made 48 in his only innings of the match. Fred Titmus, who normally batted at the tail, opened England's batting with Boycott after an injured John Edrich withdrew on the first morning. He scored 16, but was given a reprieve when Wally Grout refused to break his wicket after colliding with the bowler, Neil Hawke, while taking a run. Titmus opened with Ted Dexter in the second innings, after Boycott fractured a finger, and in partnership scored 90 for the first wicket.

322 After successfully retaining the Ashes with the only victory of the series at Headingley, Australia moved to Old Trafford and scored 8 declared for 656 – the highest total in any Test at Manchester. The foundation of the innings was a double-century opening stand from Bill Lawry (106) and Bob Simpson (311). For Simpson this was his maiden Test century, scored in his 52nd innings, and it remains the highest Test innings at Manchester and the highest by an Australian captain in England. He batted for 753 minutes, the longest innings by an Australian batsman in a Test. Tom Veivers, the Queensland right-arm off-break bowler, created Ashes history sending down a record 571 balls in England's only innings of 611. This is the only Test match where both sides scored 600 runs in the first innings.

323 The final Test match at The Oval belonged to Fred Trueman, who became the first bowler to take 300 Test wickets. Ken Barrington passed 4000 Test runs and Colin Cowdrey reached 5000, while Geoff Boycott scored his maiden Test hundred (113). Graham McKenzie finished the series with 29 wickets, at the time a record-equalling performance by an Australian bowler in England.

324 In the penultimate first-class fixture of the tour, at Hastings, all 22 players had a bowl in the match between the Australians and A.E.R. Gilligan's XI. This is the only instance in all first-class cricket of every player bowling in a match.

THE TOURISTS

R.B. Simpson (c), B.C. Booth, P.J.P. Burge, A.N. Connolly,
G.E. Corling, R.M. Cowper, A.T.W. Grout, N.J.N. Hawke,
B.N. Jarman, W.M. Lawry, G.D. McKenzie, J.W. Martin,
N.C. O'Neill, J. Potter, I.R. Redpath, R.H.D. Sellers,
T.R. Veivers.

AUSTRALIA VERSUS ENGLAND 1861-2005

THE RESULTS

TEST MATCHES	FIRST-CLASS MATCHES	ALL MATCHES
P W L D	P W L D	P W L D
5 1 0 4	30 11 3 16	35 14 3 18

1st Test Nottingham: Drawn
2nd Test Lord's: Drawn
3rd Test Leeds: Australia won by 7 wickets
4th Test Manchester: Drawn
5th Test The Oval: Drawn

1965-66
TOUR OF AUSTRALIA

325 In the tour match against New South Wales in Sydney, the MCC made six declared for 527 in its first innings. Seven batsmen scored fifties, but none a century. The highest was 93 from Middlesex batsman Eric Russell.

326 A 19-year-old Doug Walters made his debut in the first Test at Brisbane and responded with a knock of 155, becoming the fifth Australian to score a century in the first innings of his maiden Test. He scored another hundred (115) in the second Test at Melbourne, emulating Bill Ponsford's feat of centuries in his first two Tests.

327 England opened the third Test at Sydney with a 234-run first-wicket stand from Geoff Boycott (84) and Bob Barber (185) who scored his only Test-match century. The following Test at Adelaide produced a higher opening partnership, one of 244 from Bob Simpson (225) and Bill Lawry (119) – Australia's highest first-wicket stand against England at home. In England's second innings, Ken Barrington scored his 10th consecutive 50 in first-class matches at the Adelaide Oval – 104, 52, 52*, 63, 132* in 1962-63 and 69, 51, 63, 60 & 102 in 1965-66.

328 In the fifth Test at Melbourne Bob Cowper scored 307, the only triple-century in a Test match in Australia. Spanning 693 minutes, it remains the slowest triple-century in an Australian first-class match. Ken Barrington's final Test hundred against Australia was reached with a six, becoming the first player to achieve the feat twice in Ashes cricket.

329 By a remarkable coincidence, the rare feat of a bowler taking a wicket with his first ball in first-class cricket was achieved three times against the MCC during the tour. Barry Rothwell did so, dismissing Bob Barber, for New South Wales at Sydney, as did South Australia's Allan Frost (Geoff Boycott) at the Adelaide Oval and Tasmania's Kerry Flint (Peter Parfitt) at Launceston.

THE TOURISTS

M.J.K. Smith (c), D.A. Allen, R.W. Barber, K.F. Barrington,
G. Boycott, D.J. Brown, M.C. Cowdrey, J.H. Edrich,
K. Higgs, I.J. Jones, J.D.F. Larter, J.T. Murray, P.H. Parfitt,
J.M. Parks, W.E. Russell, F.J. Titmus.
(Reinforcement: B.R. Knight).

THE RESULTS

TEST MATCHES	FIRST-CLASS MATCHES	ALL MATCHES
P W L D	P W L D	P W L D
5 1 1 3	15 5 2 8	24 13 2 9

1st Test Brisbane: Drawn
2nd Test Melbourne: Drawn
3rd Test Sydney: England won by an innings and 93 runs
4th Test Adelaide: Australia won by an innings and 9 runs
5th Test Melbourne: Drawn

1968
TOUR OF ENGLAND

330 Four batsmen reached the eighties in the first Test at Manchester, but none went on to score a century – Bill Lawry (81), Doug

Walters (81 & 86), Paul Sheahan (88) and England's Basil D'Oliveira (87*).

331 The second Test at Lord's saw Australia dismissed for 78 in the first innings, their lowest total against England since 1912. Paul Sheahan batted for 52 minutes in the second innings without getting off the mark.

332 In the third Test at Edgbaston, Colin Cowdrey became the first player to appear in 100 Tests and celebrated the milestone with a hundred (104).

333 Injuries sustained at Edgbaston prevented the two captains – Bill Lawry and Colin Cowdrey – from playing in the fourth Test at Leeds. Barry Jarman and Tom Graveney were named as their replacements and made their only appearances as Test captains. England's left-arm spinner Derek Underwood made 45* batting at No.11.

334 Off-spinner Ashley Mallett made his Test debut at The Oval and dismissed Colin Cowdrey with the fifth ball of his first at No.9 he scored 43*. Derek Underwood achieved his best Test figures against Australia, bowling England to victory with 7 for 50.

THE TOURISTS

W.M. Lawry (c), I.M. Chappell, A.N. Connolly,
R.M. Cowper, E.W. Freeman, J.W. Gleeson, N.J.N. Hawke,
R.J. Inverarity, B.N. Jarman, L.R. Joslin, G.D. McKenzie,
A.A. Mallett, I.R. Redpath, D.A. Renneberg, A.P. Sheahan,
T.B. Taber, K.D. Walters.

THE RESULTS

TEST MATCHES	FIRST-CLASS MATCHES	ALL MATCHES
P W L D	P W L D	P W L D
5 1 1 3	25 8 3 14	28 9 3 16

1st Test Manchester: Australia won by 159 runs
2nd Test Lord's: Drawn
3rd Test Birmingham: Drawn
4th Test Leeds: Drawn
5th Test The Oval: England won by 226 runs

1970-2005

1970-71
TOUR OF AUSTRALIA

335 South Australia scored 9 declared for 649 in the MCC's opening first-class match of the 1970-71 tour. Their total is the highest score by any state against the MCC and included a double-century from South Australia's South African import Barry Richards (224).

336 In the first Test at Brisbane, Keith Stackpole (207), who survived a close run-out appeal when on 18, became the first batsman to score a double-century in an Ashes Test at the Gabba. After reaching 4 for 418, the Australians then lost their last seven wickets for 15 to be all out for 433. John Snow took four of the wickets, while Derek Underwood claimed three in seven deliveries without conceding a run. No England player scored a century in this match, although the occupiers of positions two, three and four in the batting order all passed 70 in the first innings – Brian Luckhurst (74), Alan Knott (73) and John Edrich (79). Bill Lawry scored a match-saving 84 in the second innings, occupying the crease for 330 minutes and soaking up 317 deliveries.

337 After four draws and one loss in the five first-class matches so far, the tourists went to Perth where Western Australia recorded their first-ever win against the MCC. Tony Mann (110) scored a century off 92 balls, while his captain, the former England Test cricketer Tony Lock scored 24* at No.11.

338 The second Test was the first to be staged at the WACA ground in Perth. Batting at No.7, Greg Chappell (108) scored a century on his Test debut, while Bill Lawry passed the milestones of 5000 Test runs and 2000 runs against England.

339 A hastily-arranged limited-overs match, played on the final scheduled day of the abandoned third Test at the MCG, was later recognised as the first one-day international. It took place at the same venue as the first-ever Test match and also resulted in an Australian victory. John Edrich (82) was adjudged Man-of-the-Match after scoring the first half-century. Ian Chappell (60) scored the first one-day international 50 for Australia.

340 In the fourth Test at Sydney, Bill Lawry carried his bat for 60* in Australia's second innings of 116. In doing so, he became the first Australian to achieve the feat in a Test at the SCG. John Snow was responsible for the 116-run scoreline, taking 7 for 40, his best Test figures against Australia.

341 In his fourth Test appearance Rod Marsh (92*) came close to notching his maiden Test century, only to be denied the chance when Bill Lawry declared the first innings closed. The fifth Test at Sydney was a late addition to the summer program after the abandoned third Test.

342 After Rod Marsh's debut in the first Test and Greg Chappell's debut in the second, the sixth Test at Adelaide saw the first appearance of Dennis Lillee, who took five wickets in his first innings. Geoff Boycott and John Edrich opened with stands of 107 and 103, becoming the third England pair to share 100-run opening partnerships in both innings of a Test v Australia.

343 After Australia had failed to secure a Test win in the five matches of the rubber so far, Bill Lawry was dropped for the seventh Test at Sydney. His batting spot was taken by fellow Victorian Ken Eastwood, who played in his one and only Test. Ian Chappell took over the captaincy, and lost his first match in charge. The opposing captain Ray Illingworth led his team from the field, after a section of the crowd displayed their anger at John Snow, who had hit tail-end batsman Terry Jenner on the head with a bouncer. England regained the Ashes in what had been the longest Test series in history. No Australian batsman was dismissed lbw in the entire series.

THE TOURISTS

R. Illingworth (c), G. Boycott, M.C. Cowdrey,
B.L. D'Oliveira, J.H. Edrich, K.W.R. Fletcher,
J.H. Hampshire, A.P.E. Knott, P. Lever, B.W. Luckhurst,
K. Shuttleworth, J.A. Snow, R.W. Taylor, D.L. Underwood,
A. Ward, D. Wilson. (Reinforcement: R.G.D. Willis).

THE RESULTS

TEST MATCHES	FIRST-CLASS MATCHES	ALL MATCHES
P W L D	P W L D	P W L D
6 2 0 4	14 3 1 10	24 10 2 12

AUSTRALIA VERSUS ENGLAND 1861-2005

1st Test Brisbane: Drawn
2nd Test Perth: Drawn
3rd Test Melbourne: Abandoned
4th Test Sydney: England won by 299 runs
5th Test Melbourne: Drawn
6th Test Adelaide: Drawn
7th Test Sydney: England won by 62 runs

1972
TOUR OF ENGLAND

344 On his Test debut, in the opening Ashes encounter at Manchester, Tony Greig (57 & 62) top-scored for England in each innings. Rod Marsh took five catches in the second innings and heightened his reputation as a handy batsman by scoring 91. Ian Chappell began his captaincy career in England with a duck – Tony Greig's first Test wicket. England won the match by 89 runs, their first victory in the opening match of a Test series against Australia since 1930.

345 After taking 6 for 31 on his first-class debut in England, in the tour match against Worcestershire, Bob Massie, the West Australian swing bowler, took 16 wickets on his Test debut at Lord's. With eight wickets in each innings, he became the first bowler to take more than 12 wickets on his Test debut, with his match-figures of 16 for 137 the best by a debutant in a Test match until 1987-88, when India's Narendra Hirwani took the record by conceding just one run less.

346 Bob Massie took another five wickets in the following Test at Trent Bridge, giving him a record 21 wickets in his first two Tests against England. For the second time in the series, Rod Marsh took five catches in an innings.

347 Derek Underwood (10-82) became only the third bowler, after Jim Laker and Fred Trueman, to take 10 wickets in a Test match against Australia at Leeds. Underwood received great assistance from a grassless pitch, the result of an attack of 'Fusarium Oxysporum' that followed torrential rain.

348 Australia's team for the fifth Test at The Oval was the first not to include a player from New South Wales. Ian and Greg Chappell, with knocks of 118 and 113 respectively, became the first brothers to score centuries in the same Test innings. For the second time in the series, after Manchester, Dennis Lillee took three wickets in four balls.

349 In the first one-day international in England, at Manchester, Dennis Amiss hit 103 – the first century scored at this level. Amiss and Keith Fletcher (60) shared the first century partnership in a one-day international.

350 British pop singer Daniel Boone, who had an international hit with 'Beautiful Sunday', co-wrote another song that made the Top 40 – 'Here Come the Aussies', recorded in London by the 1972 Australian cricket team.

THE TOURISTS

I.M. Chappell (c), G.S. Chappell, D.J. Colley, R. Edwards, B.C. Francis, J.W. Gleeson, J.R. Hammond, R.J. Inverarity, D.K. Lillee, A.A. Mallett, R.W. Marsh, R.A.L. Massie, A.P. Sheahan, K.R. Stackpole, H.B. Taber, K.D. Walters, G.D. Watson.

THE RESULTS

TEST MATCHES	FIRST-CLASS MATCHES	ALL MATCHES
P W L D	P W L D	P W L D
5 2 2 1	26 11 5 10	37 14 10 13

1st Test Manchester: England won by 89 runs
2nd Test Lord's: Australia won by 8 wickets
3rd Test Nottingham: Drawn
4th Test Leeds: England won by 9 wickets
5th Test The Oval: Australia won by 5 wickets

1974-75
TOUR OF AUSTRALIA

351 In his first Test against England, at Brisbane, Jeff Thomson took 3 for 59 and 6 for 46. Although Thomson had opened the Australian attack once before with Dennis Lillee, this opening Test match at the Gabba witnessed the birth of one of the greatest fast-bowling combinations of all time. Dennis Amiss and John Edrich both sustained fractured hands in the first innings which precluded them from appearing in the following Test at Perth.

352 A 41-year-old Colin Cowdrey was flown out to join the England team for his sixth tour of Australia. In his first Test since 1971, Cowdrey played in the WACA Test scoring 22 and 41. Fred Titmus, aged 42, also reappeared after a lengthy hiatus, playing in his first Test since 1968. Doug Walters (108) scored a century between tea and stumps on the second day, reaching his ton with a six off the last ball. David Lloyd was forced to retire in the second innings after being hit in the groin by a ball from Jeff Thomson. Greg Chappell completed seven catches in the match, a record number in Anglo-Australian Tests.

353 After winning the toss for the third time in this series, at Melbourne, Ian Chappell became the first captain to send in the opposition in successive Ashes Test matches.

354 Following scores of 6, 27, 2, 20, 8 and 2, England's captain Denness dropped himself for the fourth Test at Sydney. John Edrich found himself in hospital again after being struck in the ribs with the first delivery he faced from Dennis Lillee. In Australia's second innings, Ian Redpath (105) and Greg Chappell (144) shared a 220-run partnership for the second wicket.

355 In the fifth Test at Adelaide, Alan Knott became the second wicket-keeper to reach 200 dismissals and the second wicket-keeper to score a Test century (106*) against Australia. England's Dennis Amiss, Derek Underwood and Geoff Arnold all failed with the bat in both innings – the first time three batsmen from the same side had been dismissed for a pair in an Ashes Test. Colin Cowdrey played in his 42nd Test against Australia, eclipsing the previous record shared by Wilfred Rhodes and Jack Hobbs.

356 After just 130 runs in his first four Tests of this series, Mike Denness scored 188 in the final Test at Melbourne, beating the previous highest innings by an England captain in Australia (Andrew Stoddart's 173 at Melbourne in 1894-95). Dennis Lillee bowled only six overs after injuring his foot, while his partner Jeff Thomson was not selected after breaking down during the previous Test at Adelaide. Max Walker (8-143) became the first Australian bowler to take eight England wickets in an innings in a post-war Test match in Australia.

THE TOURISTS

M.H. Denness (c), D.L. Amiss, G.G. Arnold, J.H. Edrich,
K.W.R. Fletcher, A.W. Greig, M. Hendrick, A.P.E. Knott,
P. Lever, D. Lloyd, B.W. Luckhurst, C.M. Old,
R.W. Taylor, F.J. Titmus, D.L. Underwood, R.G.D. Willis.
(Reinforcement: M.C. Cowdrey).

THE RESULTS

TEST MATCHES	FIRST-CLASS MATCHES	ALL MATCHES
P W L D	P W L D	P W L D
6 1 4 1	15 5 5 5	23 8 9 6

1st Test Brisbane: Australia won by 166 runs
2nd Test Perth: Australia won by 9 wickets
3rd Test Melbourne: Drawn
4th Test Sydney: Australia won by 171 runs
5th Test Adelaide: Australia won by 163 runs
6th Test Melbourne: England won by an innings and 4 runs

1975
TOUR OF ENGLAND

357 The 1975 team lost the opening first-class tour match to Kent, the county's first win over the Australians since 1899. New South Wales batsman Alan Turner (156) scored a century on his first-class debut in England.

358 Bob Woolmer engineered an exceptional all-round double for the MCC v the Australians at Lord's. He scored two half-centuries (55 & 85) and became the first bowler to take a hat-trick against the Australians since Middlesex's Henry Enthoven at Lord's in 1934. It was performed on the day of Enthoven's funeral. Doug Walters (103*) scored a maiden first-class century at cricket's headquarters, while Colin Cowdrey was dismissed for a pair.

359 Australia won the first Test by an innings and 85 runs, completing their first Test victory at Birmingham. Graham Gooch made a pair on his Test debut.

360 Rick McCosker (111 & 115) scored two centuries in the match against Sussex at Hove, a feat last achieved by an Australian tourist in England in 1956, when Jim Burke made 138 and 125* against Somerset. Both of the captains, Greg Chappell (126) and Tony Greig (129*), also scored hundreds in the Sussex match.

361 Jim Higgs was no-balled for throwing in the game against Leicestershire, and completed a forgettable match when he was out to the only ball he received on the entire tour!

362 Dennis Lillee made the highest score of his first-class career in the second Test at Lord's. His 73* is the highest unbeaten Test score by an Australian No.10 batsman. David Steele, the bespectacled 33-year-old making his Test debut, dismissed Ashley Mallett with his fourth ball, while John Edrich (175), aged 38, made his highest, and last, Test century against Australia. The other highlight of the match was the debut of Michael Angelow, who became England's first Test-match streaker.

363 The third Test at Leeds was abandoned as a draw after the pitch was damaged by a group campaigning for the release of a prisoner serving 17 years for armed robbery. One of those charged over the incident, Peter Chappell, later received an 18-month jail sentence. The one player most affected by the abandonment was Rick McCosker, who was on course for a maiden Test hundred, his innings cut short on 95*.

364 In the match against the Australians at Chelmsford, Essex leg-spinner Robin Hobbs scored the fastest century of the season, and the quickest in 55 years, bringing up his hundred in just 44 minutes. His whirlwind knock included 12 fours and seven sixes.

365 England scored its highest second-innings total against Australia with 538 in the final Test at The Oval. This was the last Test match of six days duration in England.

THE TOURISTS

I.M. Chappell (c), G.S. Chappell, R. Edwards, G.J. Gilmour,
J.D. Higgs, A.G. Hurst, B.M. Laird, D.K. Lillee,
R.B. McCosker, A.A. Mallett, R.W. Marsh, R.D. Robinson,
J.R. Thomson, A. Turner, M.H.N. Walker, K.D. Walters.

THE RESULTS

TEST MATCHES				FIRST-CLASS MATCHES				ALL MATCHES			
P	W	L	D	P	W	L	D	P	W	L	D
4	1	0	3	15	8	2	5	21	12	4	5

1st Test Birmingham: Australia won by an innings and 85 runs
2nd Test Lord's: Drawn
3rd Test Leeds: Drawn
4th Test The Oval: Drawn

1976-77
TOUR OF AUSTRALIA

366 A one-off Test match staged in Melbourne to celebrate the centenary of Test cricket resulted in a fairy-tale result, with Australia beating England by exactly the same margin (45 runs) as the first Test 100 years previously. Dennis Lillee claimed 10 wickets in the match, Rod Marsh (110*) became the first Australian wicket-keeper to score a Test century against England and Derek Randall (174) scored a century on his debut against Australia. David Hookes, on his Test debut, stood out with a sparkling second-innings 56, hitting Tony Greig for five successive boundaries.

THE TOURISTS

A.W. Greig (c), D.L. Amiss, G.D. Barlow, J.M. Brearley,
G.A. Cope, K.W.R. Fletcher, A.P.E. Knott, J.K. Lever,
G. Miller, C.M. Old, D.W. Randall, M.W.W. Selvey,
R.W. Tolchard, D.L. Underwood, R.G.D. Willis, R.A. Woolmer.

THE RESULTS

TEST MATCHES	FIRST-CLASS MATCHES	ALL MATCHES
P W L D	P W L D	P W L D
1 0 1 0	2 0 1 1	2 0 1 1

Only Test Melbourne: Australia won by 45 runs

1977
TOUR OF ENGLAND

367 The 28th Australian cricket team to tour England included 13 players who had signed contracts to play in Kerry Packer's World Series Cricket.

368 After the first five first-class matches were ruined by rain the tourists were defeated at Bath, giving Somerset their first win over the Australians in 22 matches since 1893. The West Indian fast bowler Joel Garner took the wicket of Rick McCosker with his fifth ball in his first match for the English county.

369 In the second Prudential Trophy match at Birmingham, Greg Chappell (5-20) and Gary Cosier (5-18) provided the first instance of two bowlers taking five wickets in the same innings of a one-day international. Australia was dismissed for 70, after John Lever (4-29) took four wickets for two runs in 15 balls. In the following match at The Oval, Dennis Amiss (108) and Greg Chappell (125*) provided the first instance of opposing batsmen scoring centuries in a one-day international between Australia and England.

370 The first Test match at Lord's, staged to commemorate the 25-year reign of The Queen, saw Mike Brearley as the new England captain, replacing Tony Greig, who was stood down for his involvement with World Series Cricket. Bob Willis took 7 for 78 in Australia's first innings.

371 Following 120 in the first Test, Bob Woolmer scored 137 in the second Test at Manchester. This was his third and last Test century, all of which were scored against Australia. After scoring 81 and 86 on the same ground in 1968, Doug Walters hit 88, the closest he ever came to scoring a Test century in England.

372 Ian Botham made his Test debut at Nottingham, taking 5 for 75 in the first innings. Geoff Boycott returned to the England side after excluding himself for the past 30 Tests and scored 107 and 80*. Alan Knott also scored a century, his 135 being the highest innings by an England wicket-keeper against Australia. Along the way he also became the first wicket-keeper to score 4000 Test runs. Knott and Boycott shared a record-equalling 215-run partnership for the sixth wicket, with the latter becoming the first player to bat on each day of a five-day Ashes Test. England won the third Test by seven wickets, their first victory over Australia at this venue since 1930.

373 Although the match against Minor Counties at Sunderland was not first-class, the Australians continued their indifferent form with a six-wicket loss. This was the first-ever victory by Minor Counties over an Australian team.

374 England regained the Ashes at Leeds, the first time since 1886 that they had won three Tests against Australia in a series at home. Geoff Boycott (191) played a major role in the innings-victory, becoming the first batsman to score his 100th first-class century in a Test match. Ian Botham (5-21) and Mike Hendrick (4-41) dismissed Australia for 103 in the first innings – their lowest total at Leeds. Alan Knott passed the milestone of 250 dismissals, while Bob Willis took his 100th wicket.

375 With the Test series decided, Australia brought in two new players for the final match at The Oval. While Kim Hughes (1) failed on his debut, West Australian fast bowler Mick Malone celebrated his only Test appearance with 5 for 63 in his first innings. He also made his highest score with the bat (46), sharing a 100-run ninth-wicket stand with Max Walker (78*). Jeff Thomson took his 100th Test wicket, while Geoff Boycott passed 5000 Test runs and established the highest average in an Ashes series. In his three appearances, Boycott scored 107, 80*, 191, 39 and 25* for a total of 442 runs at 147.33.

376 A combination of bad weather at the start of the tour and the ensuing controversy surrounding Kerry Packer's breakaway competition ruined the summer's cricket for the players and public alike. The Australians flew home with just five first-class wins in 22 matches – one of the worst performances ever by an Australian team in England.

THE TOURISTS

G.S. Chappell (c), R.J. Bright, G.J. Cosier, I.C. Davis,
G. Dymock, D.W. Hookes, R.B. McCosker, M.F. Malone,
R.W. Marsh, K.J. O'Keeffe, L.S. Pascoe, R.D. Robinson,
C.S. Serjeant, J.R. Thomson, M.H.N. Walker, K.D. Walters.

THE RESULTS

TEST MATCHES	FIRST-CLASS MATCHES	ALL MATCHES
P W L D	P W L D	P W L D
5 0 3 2	22 5 4 13	31 8 8 15

1st Test Lord's: Drawn
2nd Test Manchester: England won by 9 wickets
3rd Test Nottingham: England won by 7 wickets
4th Test Leeds: England won by an innings and 85 runs
5th Test The Oval: Drawn

1978-79
TOUR OF AUSTRALIA

377 With Rod Marsh and Alan Knott now contracted to World Series Cricket, two new wicket-keepers made their first appearances in an Ashes series in the first Test at Brisbane. England's Bob Taylor and debutant John Maclean both took five catches in the first innings. Rodney Hogg, also on his debut, recorded what turned out to be the best figures of his Test career in this match, taking 6 for 74 in the first innings. He also made his highest score against England with 36* batting at No.11. Graham Yallop (102) scored a century in his first Test as captain, while Kim Hughes (129) took six hours to bring up his maiden Test century. Australia's first-innings total of 116 was their second-lowest in a Test match in Brisbane.

378 Western Australia suffered an embarrassing defeat at the hands of England in a three-day match at the WACA, with the home-side twice dismissed for under 100. The first-innings total of 52 was WA's lowest score against an international side and was the highest total in an Australian first-class match in which no batsman reached double figures.

379 David Gower, on his debut against Australia, scored 102 in the second Test at Perth. Rodney Hogg took 10 wickets in his second match, but finished on the losing side. For the first time since 1936-37 England recorded victories in the first two Tests of a series in Australia.

380 The third Test at Melbourne saw the debut of Allan Border, who was run out for a duck in the second innings. Rodney Hogg took his fifth haul of five wickets in six consecutive innings, bowling Australia to its only win of the summer. For Mike Brearley, this was his first loss in 16 Tests as England captain. Graeme Wood scored exactly 100, an innings that lasted 362 minutes, while England's Geoff Miller (7) took 110 minutes to score his first three runs in the first innings.

381 Geoff Boycott was dismissed first-ball, for the only time in his Test career, by Rodney Hogg, in the fourth Test at Sydney. Filling in for an exhausted John Maclean, Graham Yallop kept wicket for the last 18 overs of England's first innings and caught Ian Botham off Hogg.

382 Opening batsman Rick Darling, who made 91 at Sydney, was knocked unconscious by a ball from Bob Willis in the opening over of Australia's first innings at Adelaide. He resumed his innings the following day and scored 15. Bob Taylor scored 97 in England's second innings, his highest score against Australia.

383 The two captains, Graham Yallop and Mike Brearley, both passed the milestone of 1000 Test runs in the final match at Sydney. This was the first time England had won five Tests of a series in Australia.

384 Australia's opening bowlers, Rodney Hogg and Alan Hurst, both set Test records during the summer. Hogg completed his first Test series with 41 wickets, a record number against England in Australia, while Hurst made six noughts – the most ducks on record by a batsman in a single Test series.

THE TOURISTS

J.M. Brearley (c), I.T. Botham, G. Boycott, P.H. Edmonds,
J.E. Emburey, G.A. Gooch, D.I. Gower, M. Hendrick,
J.K. Lever, G. Miller, C.M. Old, C.T. Radley, D.W. Randall,
R.W. Taylor, R.W. Tolchard, R.G.D. Willis.

THE RESULTS

TEST MATCHES	FIRST-CLASS MATCHES	ALL MATCHES
P W L D	P W L D	P W L D
6 5 1 0	13 8 2 3	26 17 4 5

1st Test Brisbane: England won by 7 wickets
2nd Test Perth: England won by 166 runs
3rd Test Melbourne: Australia won by 103 runs
4th Test Sydney: England won by 93 runs
5th Test Adelaide: England won by 205 runs
6th Test Sydney: England won by 9 wickets

1979-80
Tour of Australia

385 Dennis Lillee hit the headlines during the first Test at Perth when he scored Test cricket's only three runs with an aluminium bat. Ten minutes of play was lost before he agreed to swap it. In the second innings, one of cricket's most memorable dismissals took place when Lillee was out for 19 – Lillee c Willey b Dilley. Two batsmen got to 99 in this match without reaching the 100-mark. Kim Hughes was the first, followed by Geoff Boycott, who became the first batsman to score 99* in a Test, and the first England batsman to carry his bat through a Test innings without scoring a hundred. Allan Border reached 1000 Test runs, while Jeff Thomson took his 150th wicket.

386 During the second Test at Sydney, Derek Underwood became the fifth England bowler to take 100 wickets against Australia. Back in the Australian side after four years, Ian Chappell reached 2000 Test runs against England. David Gower and Greg Chappell became the third and fourth batsmen in this series to reach the nineties without scoring a century. Both made identical scores in each innings – 3 and 98*.

387 Graham Stevenson, a late replacement for the tour, took 4 for 7 in 20 balls on his England debut in a one-day international at Sydney.

388 In the final Test at Melbourne, Graham Gooch (99) became the fifth batsman to finish in the nineties. Ian Botham (119*) hit his maiden Test century against Australia, Dennis Lillee took his 200th Test wicket and Greg Chappell matched his brother, Ian, by passing 2000 runs against England. Both reached the milestone in 29 Tests. Australia won the series 3-0, but the Ashes were not at stake.

THE TOURISTS

J.M. Brearley (c), D.L. Bairstow, I.T. Botham, G. Boycott,
G.R. Dilley, G.A. Gooch, D.I. Gower, M. Hendrick,
W. Larkins, J.K. Lever, G. Miller, D.W. Randall, R.W. Taylor,
D.L. Underwood, P. Willey, R.G.D. Willis.
(Reinforcements: J.E. Emburey, G.B. Stevenson).

THE RESULTS

TEST MATCHES	FIRST-CLASS MATCHES	ALL MATCHES
P W L D	P W L D	P W L D
3 0 3 0	8 3 3 2	20 10 7 3

1st Test Perth: Australia won by 138 runs
2nd Test Sydney: Australia won by 6 wickets
3rd Test Melbourne: Australia won by 8 wickets

1980

TOUR OF ENGLAND

389 In the first Prudential Trophy match at The Oval, Mike Hendrick became the first England bowler to take five wickets in a one-day international.

390 In the final first-class match before the Centenary Test at Lord's, Nottinghamshire defeated the Australians by an innings and 76 runs, the biggest victory by any county over the tourists last century.

391 The only Test match of this mini-tour was staged at Lord's to celebrate the centenary of Test cricket in England. Graham Wood (112) scored a century in his first-ever appearance at cricket's headquarters. Fellow West Australian Kim Hughes (117) also scored a hundred, becoming the first Australian to bat on all five days of a Test. In the second innings, Hughes scored a dazzling 84, punctuated by a massive six, off Chris Old, onto the top deck of the pavilion. Ten hours of the match were lost to rain and led to a section of MCC members jostling umpire David Constant on his return to the pavilion following an inspection of the pitch. This was the last Test match for veteran BBC commentator John Arlott.

THE TOURISTS

G.S. Chappell (c), A.R. Border, R.J. Bright, G. Dymock, J. Dyson, K.J. Hughes, B.M. Laird, D.K. Lillee, A.A. Mallett, R.W. Marsh, L.S. Pascoe, J.R. Thomson, G.M. Wood, G.N. Yallop.

THE RESULTS

TEST MATCHES	FIRST-CLASS MATCHES	ALL MATCHES
P W L D	P W L D	P W L D
1 0 0 1	5 1 1 2	8 1 4 3

Only Test Lord's: Drawn

1981
TOUR OF ENGLAND

392 In the third Prudential Trophy match at Headingley, Rod Marsh became the first wicket-keeper to take five catches in a one-day international.

393 Jeff Thomson was at his hostile-best in the Australia-Middlesex match at Lord's, but on this occasion it was the tourists who bore the brunt. The Queensland fast bowler was contracted to Middlesex for the season, and in the game against the Australians took 2 for 35 in the first innings, putting Graeme Wood in hospital after he was hit on the temple-guard of his helmet.

394 The first Test match at Nottingham was the first Test in England with play on a Sunday and the first five-day Test without a rest day. After 10 years and 58 Tests, Bob Willis reached the milestone of 200 wickets, while Rod Marsh became the first wicket-keeper to reach 100 dismissals in Anglo-Australian Tests. Terry Alderman took nine wickets on his Test debut, while the inclusion of Trevor Chappell in the Test line-up represented the first instance of three brothers having played Test cricket for Australia. Kim Hughes won his first Test as captain against England – Australia's first victory at Nottingham since 1948.

395 The second Test at Lord's marked the 100th appearance for the 40-year-old Geoff Boycott, and the final match for Ian Botham as captain. He ended his unhappy reign with a pair, and a record of four defeats and eight draws. Geoff Lawson took 7 for 81, his best figures against England, while Dennis Lillee had to wait an agonising 84 overs before taking his first wicket of the match.

396 England won its first Test of the series at Leeds, under its resurrected captain Mike Brearley. The 18-run victory was one of the narrowest in Ashes history, and the first this century by a team following-on (Australia 9d-401 & 111, England 174 & 356). Ian Botham, relieved of the burden of captaincy, became the first England player to score a century and take five wickets in an innings of an Ashes Test match. He blasted his way to 149*, his hundred coming off just 87 balls, and with the No.9 batsman Graham Dilley (56) in fine form, took England to 356. After commanding a 227-run lead on the first innings, Australia faced a target of just 130 for victory. Bob Willis then took career-best figures of 8 for 43 as Australia lost 9 for 55 crumbling to an all-out total of 111. Dennis Lillee passed Hugh Trumble's record of 141 wickets against England, while Rod Marsh overtook Bob Taylor's record of 263 Test dismissals.

397 Following its humiliation at Leeds, Australia won a 30-overs rain-reduced match against Scotland, under the captaincy of Rod Marsh. He scored 12 as an opening batsman, and then bowled Australia to victory taking the last three wickets, without conceding a run, in his only over.

398 The Australians' first win on the tour against a county side came at Worcester. The Australians easily reached the target of 241 at a scoring rate of 119 runs per 100 balls.

399 England completed its second successive victory in the fourth Test at Birmingham, with Ian Botham demolishing Australia in the second innings, taking 5 for 1 in 28 deliveries. For the first time in a post-war Test match, no batsman scored a half-century.

400 With Rodney Hogg and Geoff Lawson unavailable for the fifth Test at Manchester, Australia called up Mike Whitney from the obscurity of league cricket for his Test debut, after only six first-class appearances. He took four wickets and made a pair. The other debutant in this match, England's Paul Allott (52*) scored his maiden first-class fifty, off 92 balls, batting at No.10, while Chris Tavare (78) required 219 balls for his fifty. Batting with an injured finger, Allan Border made an unbeaten 123 in the second innings, his hundred taking 373 minutes for the slowest century by an Australian batsman against England. Ian Botham hit another blistering ton, his 118 including six sixes – then the most by an England batsman in a Test innings against Australia. Dennis Lillee took his 150th wicket against England, Bob Willis his 100th against Australia and Alan Knott became the first wicket-keeper to achieve 100 dismissals against Australia. Australia was dismissed for 130 in 30.2 overs in the first innings – their shortest Test innings since Birmingham 1902 – and scored 402 in the second, their highest total in losing a Test.

401 The first-wicket stand of 120 between Graeme Wood (66) and Martin Kent (54) in the final Test at The Oval was Australia's 50th opening century partnership and their first in 106 Test innings against all countries since 1976-77. Kim Hughes passed the milestone of 1000 Test runs against England, Dirk Wellham (103) scored a century on his Test debut and Geoff Boycott (137) passed Colin Cowdrey's record of 60 Test-match half-centuries. Ian Botham took his 200th wicket in Test cricket, while Terry Alderman took his 42nd wicket of the summer – a record number for an Australian bowler in a Test series against England.

402 Dirk Wellham topped both the batting and bowling averages on his first overseas tour – 497 first-class runs at 55.22 and 1 wicket at 11.00.

THE TOURISTS

K.J. Hughes (c), T.M. Alderman, G.R. Beard, A.R. Border,
R.J. Bright, T.M. Chappell, J. Dyson, R.M. Hogg,

D.K. Lillee, R.W. Marsh, S.J. Rixon, D.M. Wellham,
G.M. Wood, G.N. Yallop.
(Reinforcements: C.G. Rackemann, M.R. Whitney).

THE RESULTS

TEST MATCHES	FIRST-CLASS MATCHES	ALL MATCHES
P W L D	P W L D	P W L D
6 1 3 2	17 3 3 11	25 7 6 12

1st Test Nottingham: Australia won by 4 wickets
2nd Test Lord's: Drawn
3rd Test Leeds: England won by 18 runs
4th Test Birmingham: England won by 29 runs
5th Test Manchester: England won by 103 runs
6th Test The Oval: Drawn

1982-83
TOUR OF AUSTRALIA

403 In England's opening match on the 1982-83 tour, against Queensland, Bob Taylor made his 1528th dismissal behind the stumps in first-class cricket, passing John Murray's world wicket-keeping record. Harry Frei, on his first-class debut for Queensland, took five wickets and scored a half-century (57), off 24 balls, batting at No.8.

404 In the second match, against South Australia, England's stand-in captain Ian Botham was dismissed 'obstructing the field', but was recalled to the crease after intervention by the state captain David Hookes. England's first-innings total of 9 declared for 492 was boosted by a last-wicket stand of 112* from Eddie Hemmings (60*) and Robin Jackman (50*). This remains the highest unbeaten tenth-wicket partnership by an English pair in a first-class match in Australia.

405 England's openers Chris Tavare and Graeme Fowler were both dismissed for a duck – c Marsh b Lillee – in the match against Western Australia in Perth.

AUSTRALIA VERSUS ENGLAND 1861-2005

406 After capturing a record 42 wickets in the 1981 Ashes series, Terry Alderman claimed just one wicket in this rubber. He was forced out of the first Test in Perth after dislocating his shoulder when he tackled a spectator who'd invaded the playing area. Fast bowler Norman Cowans became England's 500th Test player, but had an undistinguished Test debut failing to take a wicket in his 16 overs. Chris Tavare remained anchored on 66 for 90 minutes in the first innings, and took 63 minutes to get off the mark in the second. Ian Botham became the first player to reach the Test double of 3000 runs and 250 wickets.

407 The second Test at Brisbane saw, for the first time, five Queensland players in an Australian Test XI. Two were making their Test debuts, the South African-born Kepler Wessels and Carl Rackemann. Wessels scored 162 in his first innings, and with 46 in the second, became the first Australian to score over 200 runs in his first Test. With 6 for 47 and 5 for 87 Geoff Lawson became the first bowler to take more than 10 wickets in an Ashes Test at the Gabba, while Rod Marsh took an Ashes-record six catches in the second innings and became the first wicket-keeper to take 300 Test catches.

408 The giant MCG electronic scoreboard was used for the first time at a cricket match during the game between Victoria and England in early December.

409 Greg Chappell (115) made his ninth and final hundred against England in the third Test at Adelaide and became the third Australian, after Clem Hill and Don Bradman, to reach the milestone of 2500 runs against England. Bob Willis became the third England captain, after Peter May and Mike Denness, to lose a Test match at Adelaide after sending Australia into bat. Both of Australia's openers, Kepler Wessels and John Dyson, were dismissed in identical fashion in the first innings – caught by Bob Taylor off Ian Botham for 44.

410 England bounced back in the fourth Test at Melbourne, claiming victory in a thriller by just three runs – England's narrowest winning margin in Australia. The 250th Test match between the two countries saw all four innings totals completed within a range of just 10 runs (England 284 & 294, Australia 287 & 288). Ian Botham reached the double of 1000 runs and 100 wickets against Australia in a record 22 matches, while Rod Marsh broke the world record for most dismissals in a Test series. Allan Border (62*) and Jeff Thomson (21) put on a spirited last-wicket stand of 70, before the latter was caught by Geoff Miller off a rebounded fumble from Chris Tavare.

411 In the final Test at Sydney, Rod Marsh took just one dismissal, extending his series total to 28 – the record for any wicket-keeper in a Test series. Marsh's counterpart, Bob Taylor also achieved a significant milestone in this match, passing the Test double of 1000 runs and 150 dismissals. Batting at No.3 in the second innings as a night-watchman, Eddie Hemmings made England's highest score in the match with 95.

412 Ian Botham was fined $400 for remarks that appeared in *The Sun* newspaper criticising the umpiring in the fifth Test. Botham also took legal action against *The Sun*, after the paper ran stories on an alleged incident with Rodney Hogg at a Sydney pub.

THE TOURISTS

R.G.D. Willis (c), I.T. Botham, G. Cook, N.G. Cowans,
G. Fowler, I.J. Gould, D.I. Gower, E.E. Hemmings,
R.D. Jackman, A.J. Lamb, V.J. Marks, G. Miller,
D.R. Pringle, D.W. Randall, C.J. Tavare, R.W. Taylor.
(Reinforcement: T.E. Jesty).

THE RESULTS

TEST MATCHES	FIRST-CLASS MATCHES	ALL MATCHES
P W L D	P W L D	P W L D
5 1 2 2	11 4 3 4	23 10 9 4

1st Test Perth: Drawn
2nd Test Brisbane: Australia won by 7 wickets
3rd Test Adelaide: Australia won by 8 wickets
4th Test Melbourne: England won by 3 runs
5th Test Sydney: Drawn

1985
TOUR OF ENGLAND

413 In the opening first-class match at Taunton, Peter Roebuck (33*) became the first post-war Somerset player to carry his bat against a touring side. Queensland wicket-keeper Ray Phillips deputised throughout most of the match for an ill Wayne Phillips, achieving seven dismissals.

414 In the 12th innings of his first-class career, Victoria's Simon O'Donnell scored 100* on his debut at Lord's in the match against the MCC. Allan Border (125) scored his third hundred in successive first-class innings. With a score of 100 in his next match, against Derbyshire, the Australian captain became the first batsman to score hundreds in the first four first-class innings of a tour of England. His dismissal for 44 in the third one-day international at Lord's was the first time Border had been dismissed for under 50 in his first eight innings.

415 Tim Robinson dominated England's first-Test victory at Leeds scoring 175 in his first match against Australia. England reached 533 in its first innings with a 49-run partnership for the last wicket from the bats of Paul Downton (54) and Norman Cowans (22*). The Australian wicket-keeper Wayne Phillips made 91 in the second innings, his highest score against England.

416 In the final warm-up match prior to the second Test the Australians fell for a dismal 76 at Southampton, their lowest total against Hampshire. An injured Wayne Phillips, batting down the order at No.11, top-scored for Australia with 15.

417 Allan Border was Australia's top-scorer in each innings of the Test match at Lord's with 196 and 41, accounting for 43 per cent of his side's runs. Ian Botham took five wickets in an innings for the 25th time in his career, while spinner Bob Holland, at the age of 38, and in his first Ashes Test, also grabbed a bag of five. Australia won the match by four wickets.

418 David Gower (166), Graeme Wood (172) and Greg Ritchie (146) all scored big hundreds in the drawn third Test at Nottingham. This was Wood's highest and last Test century against England, while for Ritchie, this was his only hundred against England.

419 Glamorgan pulverised the Australian bowlers in the tour match at Neath, with the Pakistani pair of Javed Miandad (200*) and Younis Ahmed (118*) adding a record 306 runs for the fourth wicket. This was the first occasion in Glamorgan's history that two batsmen had scored hundreds in a first-class match against a touring team.

420 Mike Gatting (160) scored his first Test century at home, and his first against Australia, in the fourth Test at Manchester. His wicket was taken by Craig McDermott, who finished the innings with 8 for 141. At the age of 20, McDermott became the youngest Australian bowler to take eight wickets in a Test innings.

421 After David Boon (206*) had registered the highest-ever score by an Australian against Northamptonshire just prior to the fourth Test, Wilf Slack, with 201*, then made the highest score by a Middlesex batsman against the Australians in the match immediately before the fifth Test. Slack and Keith Brown (102), on his debut at Lord's, shared a 213-run opening partnership, the highest by the county against an Australian team.

422 England secured an innings victory in the fifth Test at Birmingham, after Richard Ellison, the swing bowler from Kent, took 10 wickets and David Gower (215) registered his country's highest individual score at Edgbaston. In his last appearance for Australia, Jeff Thomson, now aged 35, took his 200th, and final wicket when he dismissed Graham Gooch for 19 (it was also his 100th against England). Gower and Tim Robinson (148) shared a 331-run partnership for the second wicket, while Mike Gatting scored his second hundred in successive innings, reaching 100*. This was the first time since The Oval in 1938 that three England batsmen had scored centuries in the same innings against Australia. The first three batsmen in Australia's second innings – Andrew Hilditch, Graeme Wood and Kepler Wessels – were each dismissed for 10. Allan Border reached 500 runs in the series for the second time in his career against England, becoming the first to do so since Don Bradman, who managed the feat three times. Ellison and Robinson both announced their engagements on the fourth day.

423 David Gower continued his rich form in the sixth Test at The Oval, taking part in his second successive triple-century partnership. Graham Gooch (196) scored his maiden century against Australia and shared a match-winning second-wicket stand of 351 with the England skipper, who made 157. Gower finished the series with 723 runs, the record aggregate in a Test series against Australia in England. England won the final two Tests by an innings, taking the series 3-1. This was the first time since the 1890s that England had won three consecutive series at home.

THE TOURISTS

A.R. Border (c), M.J. Bennett, D.C. Boon, D.R. Gilbert,
A.M.J. Hilditch, R.G. Holland, G.F. Lawson,
C.J. McDermott, G.R.J. Matthews, S.P. O'Donnell,
R.B. Phillips, W.B. Phillips, G.M. Ritchie, J.R. Thomson,
D.M. Wellham, K.C. Wessels, G.M. Wood.

THE RESULTS

TEST MATCHES	FIRST-CLASS MATCHES	ALL MATCHES
P W L D	P W L D	P W L D
6 1 3 2	20 4 3 13	24 6 4 14

1st Test Leeds: England won by 5 wickets
2nd Test Lord's: Australia won by 4 wickets
3rd Test Nottingham: Drawn
4th Test Manchester: Drawn
5th Test Birmingham: England won by an innings and 118 runs
6th Test The Oval: England won by an innings and 94 runs

1986-87
TOUR OF AUSTRALIA

424 In England's one-day tour-opener, against a South-East Queensland Country XI at Lawes, Allan Lamb scored an unbeaten 111, with 24 runs coming off the final over. Phil Edmonds was no-balled for throwing, after playfully chucking the ball at a batsman who had just hit him for two sixes.

425 In the match against Queensland at Brisbane, Mike Gatting dismissed Robbie Kerr with his first first-class delivery of the tour. In the second innings Ian Botham hit 87, off just 67 balls, with 11 fours and four sixes, one of which shattered a Queensland Cricket Association office window.

426 The tourists beat South Australia in Adelaide ending a 14-match sequence in which England teams had failed to gain a first-class victory. On his first-class debut in Australia, James Whitaker scored 108 in the England XI's first innings.

427 David Gower, Wilf Slack, Allan Lamb and Mike Gatting all suffered ducks in the first-class match against Western Australia, with Gower completing a pair. Geoff Marsh (124 & 63) batted for 345 minutes in the first innings, and for 245 in the second, while Chris Matthews hit eight fours and two sixes in his quick-fire 56.

428 England won the opening Test match at Brisbane, thanks in part to an Ian Botham assault. In the first innings he belted 138, including an Ashes-record 22 runs off an over from Merv Hughes. Opening the batting for the first time with David Boon, Geoff Marsh scored 56 and 110 in his first Ashes Test match. England's John Emburey took 5 for 80 in the second innings, passing the milestone of 100 Test wickets and 50 against Australia. Bruce Reid, at 6 feet 8 inches, became the tallest player to appear in an Ashes Test match. Merv Hughes, who like Reid, was appearing in his first Ashes Test, made a pair. Australia was asked to follow-on, for the first time in a Test at Brisbane, and for the second successive Ashes Test, after The Oval in 1985.

429 New South Wales defeated the England side at Newcastle, their first victory over the tourists since 1962-63. Both of the English openers, Chris Broad and Bill Athey, were out lbw for a duck in their second innings score of 82 – the lowest total by an England side in Australia since 1936-37.

430 Allan Border lost the toss for the first time in nine Tests, at Perth, and England responded with an opening partnership of 223 between Chris Broad (162) and Bill Athey (96). David Gower (136) and wicket-keeper Jack Richards (133) also scored centuries in England's highest Test total at Perth (8d-592). Border scored 125 – his 20th Test century in his 150th innings and took him past the milestone of 2000 runs against England. It was also Australia's 200th century against England. Allan Lamb, who failed with the bat in both innings (0 & 2), had several hundred dollars-worth of cash and travellers cheques stolen from his hotel room during the Test.

431 Mike Gatting arrived 20 minutes for the start of the match against Victoria, after sleeping in. The tourists claimed victory by five wickets – Victoria's first loss to an England side since 1962-63.

432 The third Test at Adelaide began with Geoff Marsh (43) and David Boon (103) sharing a 113-run first-wicket partnership – Australia's first three-figure opening against England in a home Test since 1974-75. Boon and Mike Gatting (100 & 0) both scored a century and a duck in this match, while Chris Broad (116) and Allan Border (100*) both scored their second centuries in successive Tests. Much to the delight of the Adelaide crowd and an Australia-wide TV audience, a woman took her ironing-board to the ground and ironed her clothes on the final day.

433 The England XI (9d-342) defeated Tasmania (79 & 167) by an innings and 96 runs at Hobart, a match in which John Emburey scored 46, hitting 10 fours and a six – a new world record for the highest first-class innings made up entirely of boundaries.

434 England gained an innings victory in the fourth Test at Melbourne, thus retaining the Ashes. It was the first time since the first Test in 1901-02 that England had defeated Australia within three days. Chris Broad (112) scored his third hundred in successive Ashes Tests, matching Jack Hobbs and Walter Hammond. Gladstone Small, on his Ashes debut, was named Man-of-the-Match for his seven wickets.

435 In a one-day international at Perth, Ian Botham hit Australia's Simon Davis for 26 runs (4, 4, 2, 4, 6, 6) in an over on his way to a 39-ball 68.

436 After just six first-class appearances, and only one for New South Wales in the current season, Sydney off-spinner Peter Taylor made his Test debut in the final match at the SCG. Speculation was rife that the selectors had got it wrong, inadvertently naming P.L. Taylor rather than the up-and-coming NSW opening batsman M.A. Taylor. Channel 9 even interviewed Mark Taylor asking him how he felt about his selection. Peter was the one the selectors wanted and he vindicated their decision by taking 6 for 78 in the first innings, and scoring 42 batting at No.9. Leg-spinner Peter Sleep did the damage in England's second innings with 5 for 72, giving Australia its first victory in 15 Tests.

437 Allan Lamb passed 2000 runs in one-day internationals when he scored his first run in the World Series Cup match against Australia at Sydney. He finished on 77* after hitting Bruce Reid for 2, 4, 6,

2 and 4 in the final over to give England a three-wicket victory with a ball to spare. A spectator at this match was fined $200 by a Sydney court after entering the Australian dressing-room and stealing a pad.

438 England completed the 1986-87 summer with a hat-trick of competition victories – the Ashes, the Benson & Hedges Challenge in Perth and the World Series Cup.

THE TOURISTS

M.W. Gatting (c), C.W.J. Athey, I.T. Botham, B.C. Broad, P.A.J. DeFreitas, G.R. Dilley, P.H. Edmonds, J.E. Emburey, N.A. Foster, B.N. French. D.I. Gower, A.J. Lamb, C.J. Richards, W.N. Slack, G.C. Small, J.J. Whitaker.

THE RESULTS

TEST MATCHES	FIRST-CLASS MATCHES	ALL MATCHES
P W L D	P W L D	P W L D
5 2 1 2	11 5 5 3	30 19 7 4

1st Test Brisbane: England won by 7 wickets
2nd Test Perth: Drawn
3rd Test Adelaide: Drawn
4th Test Melbourne: England won by an innings and 14 runs
5th Test Sydney: Australia won by 55 runs

1987-88
TOUR OF AUSTRALIA

439 A one-off Test match was played against England at the SCG in 1988 to commemorate Australia's Bicentenary. England opener Chris Broad (139) scored his fourth century, all at different venues, in six Tests against Australia. Upset at his dismissal by Steve Waugh, Broad smashed the leg stump with his bat and later incurred a $500 fine. The only other century-maker was Australian opening batsman David Boon, who made 184*, the same score made by Dean Jones in the previous Australia-

England encounter (Sydney 1986-87). The Sydney Test match was drawn, but Australia won the 'Bicentennial One-day International' played two days later in Melbourne.

THE TOURISTS

M.W. Gatting (c), C.W.J. Athey, B.C. Broad,
D.J. Capel, P.A.J. DeFreitas, G.R. Dilley, J.E. Emburey,
N.H. Fairbrother, N.A. Foster, B.N. French, E.E. Hemmings,
P.W. Jarvis, M.D. Moxon, N.V. Radford, C.J. Richards,
K.T. Robinson.

THE RESULTS

TEST MATCHES	FIRST-CLASS MATCHES	ALL MATCHES
P W L D	P W L D	P W L D
1 0 0 1	1 0 0 1	2 0 1 1

Only Test Sydney: Drawn

1988
TOUR OF ENGLAND

440 A team of Aborigines, managed by rugby star Mark Ella, embarked on a tour of England in 1988 – the second aboriginal side to visit Britain following the first in 1868. The squad, featuring one player with first-class experience – Mike Mainhardt – won 16 of the 28 scheduled one-day games. The captain John McGuire (110) had the distinction of scoring their first century, in the match against Farnham, while Eddie Graham-Vanderbyl made 99* in the following game, against the Sport Aid XI at Southampton. Off-spinner Bert Pearce, a grade-cricketer from Sydney, topped the bowling averages with 21 wickets.

THE TOURISTS

J. McGuire (c), S. Appoo, P. Bagshaw, D. Breckenridge,
N. Bulger, N. Fry, D. Gardner, E. Graham-Vanderbyl,

P. Gregory, G. James, M. Mainhardt, L. Marks, J. Marsh, D. Monaghan, B. Pearce, D. Thompson, M. Williams.

THE RESULTS

FIRST-CLASS MATCHES				ALL MATCHES			
P	W	L	D	P	W	L	D
–	–	–	–	27	16	10	1

1989
TOUR OF ENGLAND

441 In a one-day match against the MCC at Lord's, David Boon (166) and Geoff Marsh (102) shared an opening stand of 277, the highest in a one-day game in England involving first-class players. Marsh's hundred followed a duck in the previous match; for Boon it was his second hundred in successive one-day innings. Tom Moody smashed four sixes in his 72, while one of the three sixes struck by Allan Border (66) hit a woman spectator in the face.

442 The Australians lost the opening first-class fixture, against Worcestershire, with 24 wickets falling on the first day. The county bowlers dismissed Australia for 103 before lunch in the first innings, with Phil Newport taking 6 for 43. His match figures of 11 for 127 were the best-ever by a Worcestershire bowler against the Australians. The three-wicket victory was Worcestershire's first win against Australia.

443 The second Texaco Trophy match, at Nottingham, resulted in the first tied one-day international in England (England 5-226, Australia 8-226), and only the second worldwide.

444 Dean Jones took centre-stage in the match against Warwickshire at Birmingham, hitting the highest score of the tour. His 248 included 19 fours, and 12 sixes – a record by an Australian touring batsman in England.

445 The Australians maintained their unbeaten record against Middlesex by recording a three-wicket win at Lord's. Since their first meeting in 1878, Australia has never lost a first-class match against the London-based county.

446 David Boon scored his fifth fifty in his five matches on the tour to date, with a record-breaking 172 against Yorkshire at Leeds. His 172 off 157 balls was his third century in successive limited-overs matches and was the highest-ever one-day score by an Australian against a first-class side.

447 The first Test at Leeds, which Australia won by 210 runs, was highlighted by an effortless batting display from Steve Waugh (177*), who scored his maiden Test century. During his 309-minute stay at the crease, Waugh made 138 runs for the fifth wicket with Dean Jones (79) and 147 for the seventh wicket with Merv Hughes (71). Opening batsman Mark Taylor made 136 in his first innings against England, and with 60 in the second innings, scored a total of 196 runs – the most by an Australian batsman in his first Test in England. Man-of-the-Match Terry Alderman took 10 wickets for the first time in his Test career, while his opening partner Geoff Lawson passed the milestone of 150 Test wickets. Jack Russell did not concede a single bye in Australia's 7 declared for 601 – the highest total without a bye in a Test match at Leeds. David Gower became the first batsman to play in 100 consecutive Test innings without scoring a duck. For the first time in Tests between Australia in England, neither team selected a specialist spinner.

448 On his first-class debut in the match against the Australians at Northampton, Tony Penberthy celebrated his selection by dismissing Mark Taylor with his first ball. His elation was short-lived, however, when he was later dismissed for a pair.

449 At the conclusion of the second Test at Lord's, in which he scored 152* and 21*, Steve Waugh had taken his series aggregate to 350 runs without being dismissed. Geoff Lawson made a career-best 74 in the first innings, the highest score by an Australian No.10 batsman in England, and in partnership with Waugh put on 130 runs for the ninth wicket, an Australian record at Lord's. Terry Alderman passed two career-milestones during the match – 100 Test wickets and 800 first-class wickets. Allan Border became the first Australian captain to twice win a Test at Lord's.

450 In the third Test at Edgbaston, Dean Jones scored 157, the highest innings by an Australian batsman at Birmingham. Angus Fraser, on his Test debut, became the first England bowler to dismiss Steve Waugh (43) in this series, bringing to an end a record sequence of scores and an average of 393.00 thus far.

451 Tom Moody had a bonny time in Scotland where he scored a century (101) against the local side at Glasgow, and broke the world record for haggis-throwing at a highland games festival!

452 With a nine-wicket win in the fourth Test at Manchester, Australia regained the Ashes in England for the first time since 1934. It was Australia's 100th victory against England and their 200th win in all Tests. Jack Russell scored an unbeaten 128 in the second innings, becoming the first England player to register his maiden first-class century in a Test against Australia.

453 Australia won the fifth Test at Nottingham by an innings and 180 runs, their largest victory-margin in England. The first day was dominated by a 329-run opening partnership from Geoff Marsh (138) and Mark Taylor (219) – the highest opening stand in Ashes history. The Australian openers became the first pair to bat throughout an entire day's play in England. David Boon (73) and Allan Border (65*) continued the run-feast, Australia declaring at 6 for 602. England's reply began in disastrous fashion, losing its opening pair of Tim Curtis for two and Martyn Moxon for a duck, with Mike Atherton, the No.3, also failing to score.

454 In the final county match of the tour, against Essex at Chelmsford, Steve and Mark Waugh made history, becoming the first twins to each hit a century in a first-class match for opposing sides. Both hit a neat 100*, Steve for the Australians, Mark for Essex. Australia's two wicket-keepers, Tim Zoehrer and Ian Healy, opened the second innings of the match with a stand of 89, Zoehrer making 93, his highest score of the summer. Zoehrer, a part-time leggie, was given a bowl for the first time on tour and dismissed Brian Hardie, topping the Australian first-class bowling averages (1 wicket at 9.00).

455 Australia made 468 in the sixth Test at The Oval, passing 400 in the first innings of all six Tests in the series. Dean Jones (122) scored his third Test century against England and passed 1000 runs against England in his 20th innings. England was defeated 4-0 and used 29 different players throughout the series, compared to Australia's 12.

456 Australia scored a total of 3877 runs in the six Tests, the highest number ever made in an Ashes series. For the first time in Ashes history, three batsmen from one side topped the 500-mark in a series – Mark Taylor (839), Dean Jones (566) and Steve Waugh (506). England's Robin Smith joined the elite group with 553 runs – the first time four batsmen had scored 500 runs in an Ashes rubber. Taylor's aggregate is the highest number of runs by an opening batsman in any Test series. Waugh, who scored his runs at 3.76 per over, emulated Don Bradman by finishing an Ashes series with an average of over 100 (126.50).

457 With 41 wickets, Terry Alderman became the first and only bowler to twice take 35 wickets in a Test series. He took five wickets an innings six times during the summer, a record in Ashes cricket.

458 Not once during the series did England establish an opening stand of 50; the highest, 35, between Graham Gooch and Chris Broad, coming in the first innings of the first Test at Headingley – 35 & 17 Leeds, 31 & 0 at Lord's, 17 at Birmingham, 23 & 10 at Manchester, 1 & 5 at Nottingham and 1 & 20 at The Oval. Five different combinations of opening batsmen were tried, with an average first-wicket partnership of just 13 for the entire series.

459 Britain's Independent Advertising Council investigated a complaint concerning an outdoor ad for Castlemaine XXXX beer and the Australian cricketers that breached standard guidelines, by featuring a person under the age of 25 – Steve Waugh.

THE TOURISTS

A.R. Border (c), T.M. Alderman, D.C. Boon,
G.D. Campbell, I.A. Healy, T.V. Hohns, M.G. Hughes,
D.M. Jones, G.F. Lawson, G.R. Marsh, T.B.A. May,
T.M. Moody, C.G. Rackemann, M.A. Taylor, M.R.J. Veletta,
S.R. Waugh, T.J. Zoehrer.

THE RESULTS

TEST MATCHES				FIRST-CLASS MATCHES				ALL MATCHES				
P	W	L	D	P	W	L	D	P	W	L	D	T
6	4	0	2	20	12	1	7	31	20	3	7	1

1st Test Leeds: Australia won by 210 runs
2nd Test Lord's: Australia won by 6 wickets
3rd Test Birmingham: Drawn

4th Test Manchester: Australia won by 9 wickets
5th Test Nottingham: Australia won by an innings and 180 runs
6th Test The Oval: Drawn

1990-91
Tour of Australia

460 England batted with just 10 players in the match against South Australia after Graham Gooch withdrew on the second day to undergo an operation on a poisoned finger. SA batted first and built a commanding first-innings total of 6 declared for 431 with Glenn Bishop (154) and Paul Nobes (131) sharing a second-wicket partnership of 275 – a state record against England. The tourists made 217 and following-on reached 325, with Denis Hickey becoming the first South Australian bowler to take four wickets in five balls.

461 Allan Lamb hit 154 and 105 against an Australian XI in Hobart, becoming the first England batsman to score two centuries in a first-class match in Australia since Peter May in 1958-59.

462 The first Test match at Brisbane was a low-scoring affair, in which no side reached 200 (England 194 & 114, Australia 152 & 0-157). Australia's opening bowlers, Terry Alderman and Bruce Reid, took 13 of England's 20 wickets, while the opening batsmen Geoff Marsh and Mark Taylor guided Australia to victory with an undefeated first-wicket stand of 157. Allan Lamb captained England in the absence of Graham Gooch, and passed the twin-milestones of 25,000 first-class runs and 4000 Test runs. For the Australian captain Allan Border, the first innings of the match was his 200th in Test cricket. His 200th innings in one-day internationals came three weeks later, also against England in Brisbane.

463 Doug Walters captained the Sir Donald Bradman Invitation XI against England at Bowral. Darren Lehmann (112*) and Michael Bevan (51*) shared a match-winning fourth-wicket partnership of 120 in 58 minutes.

Australia versus England 1861-2005

464 The second Test match at the MCG belonged to the lanky West Australian fast bowler Bruce Reid, who became the seventh Australian bowler to take 13 wickets in a Test. He twice bettered his previous-best bowling figures taking 6 for 97 and 7 for 51. Jack Russell became the first England wicket-keeper to take six catches in an innings against Australia, while Ian Healy became the sixth Australian to take five in an innings against England. David Boon and Geoff Marsh both passed 1000 Test runs against England and David Gower, 3000 runs against Australia. His first-innings' 100 was his first half-century in five Tests so far at the MCG and his nought in the second ended a Test-record run of 119 innings against all countries without a duck. Allan Border captained Australia for a record 20th time, overtaking Don Bradman.

465 The drawn third Test at Sydney was notable for the slow scoring of Mike Atherton and Carl Rackemann. The England opener's first Test century against Australia took 424 minutes, the slowest in Ashes history and the slowest in a first-class match at the SCG. In the second innings, Rackemann took 72 minutes to score his first run, setting a new record for Australia in Test cricket. David Gower (123) hit his first first-class century in Sydney and became the second England batsman to score 8000 Test runs. Allan Border passed 3000 Test runs against England, while Mark Taylor, in his 17th innings, reached 1000 runs against England.

466 England won its only first-class match of the tour when it beat Queensland by 10 wickets at Carrara, saving Graham Gooch the embarrassment of becoming the first English captain to complete a tour of Australia without a first-class victory. England's triumph on the field was, however, slightly overshadowed by David Gower and John Morris, who hired a Tiger Moth aeroplane and flew it over the ground.

467 After 100 first-class matches and 7500 runs, Mark Waugh was finally given his chance at Test level for the fourth match at Adelaide and became the 15th Australian to score a century (138) on his debut. His inclusion in the third Test line-up was at the expense of his brother Steve – they became the 11th pair of brothers to have represented Australia at Test level and were the first twins to play Test cricket. Graham Gooch (117) scored his first Test century in Australia and shared a 203-run opening partnership with Mike Atherton (87) in the second innings – England's first double-century opening stand in a Test at Adelaide. Mark Taylor had a disappointing time scoring 5 and 4, run out in both innings.

468 Craig McDermott (8-97) took his second career-haul of eight wickets in an innings against England in the fifth Test at Perth.

With another three wickets in the second innings, McDermott took 10 wickets in a Test for the first time and passed the milestone of 50 wickets against England in his 10th appearance. His opening partner, Terry Alderman, in his 17th Ashes match, took his 100th, and final, Test wicket against England. Thirty-six, or more than a third, of his 100 scalps were taken lbw.

THE TOURISTS

G.A. Gooch (c), M.A. Atherton, M.P. Bicknell, A.R.C. Fraser,
D.I. Gower, E.E. Hemmings, A. J. Lamb, W. Larkins,
C.C. Lewis, D.E. Malcolm, J.E. Morris, K.C. Russell,
G.C. Small, R.A. Smith, A.J. Stewart, P.C.R. Tufnell.
(Reinforcements: P.A.J. DeFreitas, H. Morris, P.J. Newport).

THE RESULTS

TEST MATCHES	FIRST-CLASS MATCHES	ALL MATCHES
P W L D	P W L D	P W L D
5 0 3 2	11 1 5 5	28 8 14 6

1st Test Brisbane: Australia won by 10 wickets
2nd Test Melbourne: Australia won by 8 wickets
3rd Test Sydney: Drawn
4th Test Adelaide: Drawn
5th Test Perth: Australia won by 9 wickets

1993
TOUR OF ENGLAND

469 Australia began the 1993 tour with five consecutive wins. In the match against Somerset at Taunton, Michael Slater (122) scored a century in his maiden first-class innings in England, while the captain Allan Border (54) passed the milestone of 24,000 first-class runs. On the final day, Craig McDermott was involved in an animated confrontation with his captain who had asked the fast bowler to change ends after conceding three no-balls in an over. Border's altercation was recorded by a nearby television microphone and relayed around the world: 'F-ing do that again and you will be on the next plane home, son.'

470 Australia clinched the one-day international series with a win in the second match at Birmingham, despite a record-breaking hundred from Robin Smith. He hit an unbeaten 167, the highest innings by an England batsman in one-day internationals, with 20 runs (2, 2, 6, 0, 4, 6) off Paul Reiffel's final over.

471 In the match against Surrey at The Oval, Australia's back-up wicket-keeper Tim Zoehrer equalled the Australian record of eight dismissals in a first-class innings. His six catches and two stumpings in the second innings was one shy of the world record. Mark Waugh (178) scored one of the season's fastest centuries, reaching 100 in 123 balls, and hitting, in all, 108 runs in boundaries. His onslaught included eight sixes, a feat he emulated later in the tour, against Glamorgan at Neath.

472 For the first Ashes clash at Manchester, two New Zealand-born players made their Test debuts – Andy Caddick for England, and Brendon Julian for Australia. Peter Such took 6 for 67 in the first innings – the best figures by an England bowler on his debut against Australia last century. Mark Taylor (124), who passed 10,000 first-class runs, and debutant Michael Slater (58) scored a century opening partnership in their first outing at Test level. Ian Healy scored 102* in the second innings, becoming the first Australian to score a maiden first-class century in a Test match since Harry Graham, 100 years earlier at Lord's. His sixth-wicket partnership of 180* with Steve Waugh (78*) is a record for Australia v England at Manchester. Graham Gooch (133) scored a century in England's second innings, and then became the first England batsman to be dismissed 'handled the ball'. The most memorable moment of the match came when Shane Warne completely bamboozled Mike Gatting, bowling him with his first delivery in a Test match in England. He was the fifth bowler to take a wicket with his first ball in an Ashes Test, but the first to bowl a batsman with his first delivery.

473 In the first innings of the second Test, Mark Taylor (111) and Michael Slater (152) put on 260 for the first wicket – a record opening partnership in an Ashes Test at Lord's. David Boon (164*) scored his first Test hundred in England, providing the first instance of Australia's first three batsmen all scoring centuries in the same innings of a Test match in England. Had Mark Waugh (99) scored one more run, it would have been the first occasion in all Test cricket that the top four had scored hundreds. Mike Atherton joined Mark Waugh in scoring 99, the first time two batsmen had fallen one short of a century in the same Test match at Lord's. Wicket-keeper Alec Stewart did not concede a bye during Australia's 4 declared for 632 – the highest innings total that's free of a bye in a Test match in England. Australia's victory was its first by an innings margin at Lord's and it confirmed their complete dominance at cricket's headquarters last century. England's only win at Lord's remains the distant 1934 success – 22 previous contests saw Australia winning 10 with 12 draws. This was England's 15th Test against Australia without a win – now their longest spell without success, overtaking the 14 matches between 1946-47 and 1950-51.

474 Michael Slater (111) scored a century before lunch on the first day of the match against Combined Universities at Oxford. He was the first Australian batsman to perform this feat in England since 1964, when Bob Cowper (110) made 100* against T.N. Pearce's XI at Scarborough.

475 After his blazing century in the one-day international at Birmingham, Robin Smith scored another huge hundred, this time for Hampshire. In the first innings – he was out for a duck in the second – Smith hit 191 in 236 minutes, with 32 fours and four sixes. Two sixes came off consecutive deliveries from Allan Border – both balls were never seen again and resulted in the unusual sight of the Australian captain using three different balls for three consecutive deliveries in his over.

476 England went into the third Test at Nottingham with one of its most inexperienced bowling attacks, opening with two Test debutants – the Australian-raised Martin McCague and Mark Ilott. Two batsmen also made their England debuts – opener Mark Lathwell and Graham Thorpe (114*), who became the first player to make a century on his Test debut for England since 1973. Ian Healy made his 50th dismissal against England in his 50th Test.

477 After conceding 113 runs in 20 overs on the first day of the match against Derbyshire, New South Wales bowler Wayne Holdsworth took four wickets for nought in eight balls, becoming the first Australian tourist to take a hat-trick in England since 1912. Earlier in the match, Kim Barnett (114) had become the first English-born Derbyshire player to score a century against an Australian touring team.

478 In the match against lowly-fancied Durham, the Australians, dismissed for 221, were forced to follow-on for the only time on tour. This was the final first-class match for Ian Botham who kept wicket in the final over, minus pads and gloves.

479 Australia retained the Ashes in the fourth Test after scoring a mammoth 4 declared for 653. It was the highest total ever made at Leeds and the second score of 600 by Australia at Leeds in successive visits. For the second time in this series, after Lord's, Australia recorded an emphatic victory losing just four wickets to England's 20. Allan Border hit his first Ashes century in six years, reaching 200*. It was his highest score against England and was the first Test-match double-century by a captain at Leeds. During his innings, he passed Greg Chappell's record of 24,535 first-class runs, becoming Australia's second-highest run-scorer after Don Bradman. Steve Waugh (157*) posted his third century against England – all unbeaten and all in excess of 150 – and in partnership with Border scored 332* for the fifth wicket, Australia's best for that wicket in England. David Boon (107) scored his 50th first-class century, his third in successive Test matches, and reached the milestone of 1000 Test runs in England.

480 In the fifth Test Mark Waugh (137) scored Australia's 10th Test century of the series, sharing a record fifth-wicket partnership at Birmingham of 153 with Steve Waugh (59) – the first twins to experience a century stand in Test-match cricket. In the second innings Mark (62*) recorded his fifth century partnership in five consecutive Tests with David Boon (38*). Allan Border passed another important milestone, becoming the first player to bat in 250 Test innings.

481 Mark Taylor took his first wicket in first-class cricket, in his 145th match, bowling Kent's Richard Davis at Canterbury. During his innings of 31, Queenslander Matthew Hayden became the first Australian batsman to score 1000 first-class runs on a tour of England without playing in a Test.

482 Michael Slater scored his first pair in first-class cricket in the match against Essex at Chelmsford. Wicket-keeper Tim Zoehrer played in this match as a bowler, taking three wickets in each innings to head Australia's first-class tour bowling averages (12 wickets at 20.83), repeating his extraordinary feat of the 1989 tour. Mark Waugh (108) scored his fourth first-class century of the tour, and in the process recorded an unusual double. In the corresponding match on Australia's 1989 tour, Waugh had also scored a century (100*), but on that occasion it was for Essex.

483 England defeated Australia in the final Test at The Oval, recording their first Ashes win since Melbourne 1986-87. It brought to an end a record run of 18 Tests against Australia without a victory. Graham Gooch, who resigned as England captain after the fourth Test, scored two half-centuries and passed David Gower as England's leading run-scorer. Ian Healy took his 50th first-class tour dismissal during the match and ended the Ashes rubber with 26 dismissals. He also scored 296 runs in the Tests at an average of 59.20.

484 For the second Ashes series in a row in England, four batsmen scored 500 runs – Graham Gooch (673), Mike Atherton (553), David Boon (555) and Mark Waugh (550). Atherton's aggregate was the highest number of runs in a Test series without a century.

485 Shane Warne took 34 wickets, a record for a leg-spinner in a Test series in England, while Tim May claimed 21 – their combined effort of 55, a new record for a spin pair in England, beating the 53 wickets taken by Bill O'Reilly (28) and Clarrie Grimmett (25) in 1934.

THE TOURISTS

A.R. Border (c), D.C. Boon, M.L. Hayden, I.A. Healy,
W. J. Holdsworth, M.G. Hughes, B.P. Julian,
C.J. McDermott, D.R. Martyn, T.B.A. May, P.R. Reiffel,
M.J. Slater, M.A. Taylor, S.K. Warne, M.E. Waugh,
S.R. Waugh, T.J. Zoehrer.

THE RESULTS

TEST MATCHES	FIRST-CLASS MATCHES	ALL MATCHES
P W L D	P W L D	P W L D
6 4 1 1	21 10 2 9	30 18 3 9

1st Test Manchester: Australia won by 179 runs
2nd Test Lord's: Australia won by an innings and 62 runs
3rd Test Nottingham: Drawn
4th Test Leeds: Australia won by an innings and 148 runs
5th Test Birmingham: Australia won by 8 wickets
6th Test The Oval: England won by 161 runs

1994-95
TOUR OF AUSTRALIA

486 A day-night match played against Western Australia in Perth was the world's first limited-overs game played in 'quarters'. Both teams batted for 25 overs, and then repeated the format to complete the 50. Western Australia (5-248) won the experimental match, defeating the England XI (197) by 51 runs.

487 Two Zimbabwean-born batsmen played well in the Western Australia-England XI four-day match at the WACA – Graeme Hick (172), who scored his 78th first-class century, and WA's Murray Goodwin, who, on his first-class debut, came close to scoring his first century (91).

488 Graeme Hick revived memories of one of cricket's most famous dismissals – Lillee c Willey b Dilley – when he lost his wicket in the match against South Australia. In the first innings, the England No.3 was dismissed for 101 by Denis Hickey: Hick, hit wicket b Hickey.

489 In the Prime Minister's XI match at Canberra, both of the wicket-keepers recorded five dismissals. Mark Atkinson took five catches, while England's Steve Rhodes achieved three catches and two stumpings.

490 Greg Blewett and Matthew Hayden, who opened the batting for an Australian XI against England at Hobart, were both born on the same day – 29 October 1971.

491 In the opening Test match at Brisbane, Shane Warne took three wickets in four balls, the 10th instance of the feat in Anglo-Australian Test cricket. His second-innings haul of 8 for 71 is the best by an Australian bowler in a Test match at Brisbane, while his match analysis of 11 for 110 is a record for Australia v England at Brisbane. David Boon reached 2000 runs against England, while Mark Waugh (140) achieved his 50th first-class century and Ian Healy took his 200th Test catch.

492 Mike Gatting was out to the first ball of the one-day match against the Australian Institute of Sport Cricket Academy XI at North Sydney Oval. Alec Stewart suffered a similar fate in the following day's match. The youngsters totally embarrassed the England XI, winning both matches.

493 After a double-century opening stand from Trevor Barsby (101) and Matthew Hayden (119), Queensland lost its match to England at Toowoomba, dismissed for 314 in pursuit of 352. Mike Gatting (203*) scored England's only double-century of the tour, while Queensland's Andrew Symonds (108*) and Jimmy Maher (100*) shared an unbroken fifth-wicket partnership of 205 for the fifth wicket in the first innings.

494 During his first-innings haul of 6 for 64 in the second Test at Melbourne, Shane Warne passed the milestone of 150 wickets and 50 against England. In the second innings he bowled Australia to victory with his last three balls – the first hat-trick in Australia-England Tests since 1903-04. The only century of the match came off the bat of David Boon (131), who scored his 20th Test hundred – his first at the MCG.

495 The 50th Test between Australia and England at the SCG was highlighted by an innings from Graeme Hick. Facing a maiden Ashes century, he was left stranded on 98* when his captain, Mike Atherton, declared England's second innings at 2 for 255. Hick became the first England batsman to remain not-out in the nineties following a declaration. Set 449 runs for a record victory, Australia began with a double-century opening partnership; Michael Slater (103) and Mark Taylor (113) becoming the first pair of Australian openers to score centuries in the same Test innings at the SCG. The spin-twins Shane Warne (36*) and Tim May (10*) played out the final 113 balls in an eighth-wicket stand of 52 to secure a memorable draw.

496 Despite injuries to a number of their key players, England pulled off its only Test victory of the series at the Adelaide Oval. Mike Gatting scored his final Test century (117), and his first since 1987. It was a nerve-racking experience for him, and the crowd, spending 31 minutes on 99. The other hundred in the match was scored by Greg Blewett (102*), who became the first South Australian Test debutant to score a century at the Adelaide Oval.

497 The final Test of the series, at the WACA, was the 150th Test match between the two countries in Australia. Two of England's stalwarts Graham Gooch and Mike Gatting made their final Test appearances, while Mark Ramprakash played in his first first-class match in Australia. Steve Waugh became the first Australian batsman to finish a Test match on 99* after his twin brother Mark, acting as a runner for the injured No.11 Craig McDermott, was run out. Greg Blewett, with 115, became the fifth batsman to score centuries in his first two Tests.

498 Michael Slater scored a total of 623 Test runs, a record aggregate for an Australian opening batsman in a five-match Ashes series in Australia.

499 Ian Healy became the first wicket-keeper in Test history to achieve 24 dismissals in three consecutive series against the same opposition – 24 in 1990-91, 26 in 1993 and 25 in 1994-95.

500 As many as 22 players appeared for the England side on this tour with six called up as reinforcements for the injured. Angus Fraser, Mark Ilott, Jack Russell, Neil Fairbrother, Chris Lewis and Mark Ramprakash were called on to replace Martin McCague (injured shin), Joey Benjamin (heat rash), Alec Stewart (broken finger), Craig White (abdominal strain), Barren Gough (injured foot), Shaun Udal (side injury) and Graeme Hick (disc problem).

THE TOURISTS

M.A. Atherton (c), J.E. Benjamin, J.P. Crawley,
P.A.J. DeFreitas, M.W. Gatting, G.A. Gooch, D. Gough,
G.A. Hick, M.J. McCague, D.E. Malcolm, S.J. Rhodes,
A.J. Stewart, G.P. Thorpe, P.C.R. Tufnell, S.D. Udal,
C. White. (Reinforcements: N.H. Fairbrother, A.R.C. Fraser,
M.C. Ilott, C.C. Lewis, M.R. Ramprakash, R.C. Russell).

THE RESULTS

TEST MATCHES	FIRST-CLASS MATCHES	ALL MATCHES
P W L D	P W L D	P W L D
5 1 3 1	11 3 4 4	24 9 11 4

1st Test Brisbane: Australia won by 184 runs
2nd Test Melbourne: Australia won by 295 runs
3rd Test Sydney: Drawn
4th Test Adelaide: England won by 106 runs
5th Test Perth: Australia won by 329 runs

1997

TOUR OF ENGLAND

501 Australian skipper Mark Taylor began the campaign against county sides with an innings of 76 and a 17-run win in a limited-overs match against Northamptonshire. The final four in the Australian line-up – Brendon Julian, Shane Warne, Michael Kasprowicz and Jason Gillespie – each scored one run.

502 Medium-pacer David Leatherdale took 5 for 10 as the Australians managed just 121 in a 50-overs match against Worcestershire. Playing their third limited-overs game in four days since arriving, the Australians suffered a five-wicket loss and had to bring in a lorry to help dislodge the team bus that had become bogged on a grassed area adjacent to the cricket ground.

503 A teenaged Ben Hollioake made his one-day international debut for England at Lord's, with the 19-year-old hitting 63 from 48 balls, an innings laced with 11 fours and a six. His brother Adam hit the winning runs for the third time in succession, with England winning all three of the one-day internationals against Australia by the exact same margin of six wickets.

504 A 21-year-old Nick Trainor completed a maiden first-class century when he opened the batting for Gloucestershire in its four-day match at Bristol. Coming into the match haunted by a spell of three consecutive ducks, Trainor scored 121 with 17 fours. Mark Taylor made a duck in the first innings, while Matthew Elliott (124) and Justin Langer (152*) made hundreds in the second.

505 Victoria's Dean Jones captained Derbyshire to its first victory over an Australian XI since they beat the Imperial Forces in 1919. Chris Adams was fined £750 for disputing an lbw decision that went against him in the first innings, while his 91 in the second helped pave the way for Derbyshire reaching its victory target of 371 from 69 overs. It was the county's highest fourth-innings total in first-class cricket, and highest against an Australian XI.

506 After losing the one-day international series 3-0, Australia (118) slumped to 8 for 54 during the opening session of the first Test at Birmingham. Nasser Hussain (207) and Graham Thorpe (138) added a record 288 for the fourth wicket, with England declaring its first innings closed at 9 for 478. Australia then came within one run of matching the England total, with Mark Taylor silencing his many critics by producing a captain's knock of 129. Taylor had not scored a fifty in his previous 21 Test innings and shared in a 194-run stand with Greg Blewett (125), who became the first batsman to score hundreds in his first three Ashes Tests. After scoring a duck in the first innings, Ian Healy made amends behind the stumps gobbling up six catches and equalling Rod Marsh's Ashes record of most dismissals in an innings.

507 Glenn McGrath dismissed New Zealander Nathan Astle for 99 in Nottinghamshire's total of 239 at Trent Bridge, while the newly-arrived Paul Reiffel took three wickets in his 10-over spell. Matthew Elliott (127) and Steve Waugh (115) chipped in with centuries in the drawn three-day affair.

508 In the tour match at Grace Road, Leicester, James Ormond, appearing in only his fourth match for Leicestershire claimed 6 for 54, his first five-wicket haul in first-class cricket. Paul Reiffel was the pick of the Australian attack in the first innings with 3 for 12 off 10 overs, having taken 3 for 15 off 10 against Nottinghamshire just a few days previously.

509 Rain played a decisive role in the second Test at Lord's that brought to an end Australia's run of 18 consecutive Tests without a draw. Glenn McGrath destroyed England in the first innings with 8 for 38, as the home-side slid to an all-out total of 77. McGrath's haul was the best return in Ashes Test matches at the home of cricket, with England's total its worst at Lord's since 1888.

510 Representing Hampshire, Queenslander Matthew Hayden (6 & 2) was dismissed for a pair of single-figure scores in the tour match at Southampton, with the Australians posting an emphatic victory over Hampshire by an innings and 133 runs. Hayden was awarded his county cap by Hampshire on the second morning and needing 95 runs to become the first batsman to reach 1000 first-class runs for the season in England was bowled by Jason Gillespie for two.

511 Dean Headley, who took four wickets in each innings on his Test debut at Manchester, provided the first instance of three generations of the same family playing Test cricket, with grandfather George and his father Ron both having played for the West Indies. Alec Stewart claimed six catches in Australia's first innings and added two more in the second for a record haul of eight dismissals by an England wicket-keeper against Australia. His counterpart Ian Healy became the third keeper in

Ashes Test matches, after Rod Marsh and Alan Knott, to reach the milestone of 100 dismissals. After scoring a duck in his previous Test innings, at Lord's, Steve Waugh bounced back with 108 and 116, becoming the first right-handed batsman to score a century in each innings of an Ashes Test, and the third overall to do so, after Warren Bardsley, at The Oval in 1909, and Arthur Morris, at Adelaide in 1946-47.

512 Batsmen Justin Langer, Michael Slater and Ricky Ponting took four wickets between them as the Australians used nine bowlers in its nine-run win over a Minor Counties XI at Jesmond. Ponting actually achieved more wickets (2) than runs (1), while all-rounder Brendon Julian, batting at No.4, scored a 79-ball century (106), blasting six sixes in the final 10 deliveries.

513 Three 'young guns', each playing in their debut Ashes series, starred for Australia in its innings-and-61 run victory in the fourth Test at Headingley. A 25-year-old Matthew Elliott fell one run short of a double-century, while Ricky Ponting, aged 22, marked his first Ashes appearance with a maiden Test hundred (127), the two combining for a 268-run fifth-wicket partnership. A 22-year-old Jason Gillespie was named Man-of-the-Match after taking 7 for 37 in the first innings, the best Test figures by an Australian at Leeds. After scoring an unbeaten 54 at No.9 in Australia's 9 declared for 501, Paul Reiffel then took 5 for 49.

514 Two sets of brothers appeared in the fifth Test at Nottingham, with the Australian-bred Adam and Ben Hollioake making their Test debuts. Ben, aged 19 years and 269 days, became the youngest England Test player on debut since Brian Close, at 18 years 149 days, in 1949. During the first innings, the Hollioakes featured in a fraternal first in Test-match cricket, when they bowled in tandem to Australia's Mark and Steve Waugh.

515 Six Kent batsmen were dismissed for a first-innings duck in the Australians' final county match at Canterbury. Michael Kasprowicz dismissed the top three in the batting order for nought, while Brett Lee's brother Shane – called into the squad from Lancashire League cricket – dismissed the final three in the line-up for a duck.

516 With the Ashes retained, Australia lost the sixth Test by 19 runs, the first three-day Test match at The Oval since 1957. Graham Thorpe, with 62, was the only batsman to score a half-century in the four innings, while Tasmanian all-rounder Shaun Young was called up from county cricket with Gloucestershire and marked his only Test match with a duck in his debut innings and no wickets.

AUSTRALIA VERSUS ENGLAND 1861-2005

517 Ian Healy reached the target of 25 dismissals behind the stumps for the third Ashes series in a row, finishing with 27. Glenn McGrath was the only bowler from either side to take 25 wickets in the series, going on to capture 36 at an average of 19.47. He targeted the England skipper Mike Atherton with precision, dismissing him seven times out of 11.

THE TOURISTS

M.A. Taylor (c), M.G. Bevan, A.J. Bichel, G.S. Blewett, M.T.G. Elliott, A.C. Gilchrist, J.N. Gillespie, I.A. Healy, B.P. Julian, M.S. Kasprowicz, J.L. Langer, G.D. McGrath, R.T. Ponting, M.J. Slater, S.K. Warne, M.E. Waugh, S.R. Waugh. (Reinforcements: D.S. Berry, S. Lee, P.R. Reiffel, S. Young).

THE RESULTS

TEST MATCHES	FIRST-CLASS MATCHES	ALL MATCHES
P W L D	P W L D	P W L D NR
6 3 2 1	16 6 3 7	27 10 7 8 2

1st Test Birmingham: England won by 9 wickets
2nd Test Lord's: Drawn
3rd Test Manchester: Australia won by an innings and 133 runs
4th Test Leeds: Australia won by an innings and 61 runs
5th Test Nottingham: Australia won by 264 runs
6th Test The Oval: England won by 19 runs

1998-99
TOUR OF AUSTRALIA

518 England won the tour-opener by the narrowest of margins, defeating an ACB Chairman's XI in a festival match at Lilac Hill near Perth. The one-run victory came off the final ball of the 50-overs match in front of a crowd that numbered some 11,000.

519 After 18 months away from the game due to chronic fatigue syndrome, West Australian fast bowler Matthew Nicholson marked his return to first-class cricket by achieving a first-innings haul of 7 for 77 and scoring a maiden half-century (58*) in the tour match against the Englishmen at Perth.

520 Graham Thorpe, with 223*, and Mark Ramprakash, with an unbeaten 140, put on 377 for the fifth wicket against South Australia in Adelaide, a record for any wicket in Australia by a touring team, beating a second-wicket 368 by the MCC's Wilfred Rhodes (210) and 'Jack' Russell (201), also against South Australia at Adelaide, in 1920-21.

521 Darren Gough got into the action quickly on the opening day of the match against Queensland in Cairns, breaking one of Matthew Hayden's fingers with the second ball of the match. Play was held up during the over to repair the bowler's run-up with sawdust obtained from a nearby hardware store after none was found at the ground. Gough finally completed his over 25 minutes after it started, one of the longest overs on record that didn't include a rain-break.

522 Mark Taylor went 51 Tests at home before he made his first duck, a misfortune he suffered in his 100th Test, at the hands of England's Dominic Cork at Brisbane. It was Taylor's only duck in a Test match in Australia and came a decade after making his Test debut. Steve Waugh (112) scored his sixth century against England, but his first on home soil against the old enemy, while Ian Healy (134) became the first Australian wicket-keeper to score four Test centuries. Mark Butcher came into the Test match with a mere nine runs (0 retired hurt, 2, 5, 2, 0) in five first-class innings on tour and responded with 116, while his opening partner Mike Atherton fell for a duck.

523 Ian Healy held five catches in the first innings of the second Test at Perth, and when he caught Alex Tudor in the second broke Rod Marsh's world record of 343 catches. Tudor took the most wickets for England on his Test debut, 4 for 89 and 1 for 19.

524 After their wicket-keeping captain Alec Stewart scored a century (126) in the tour match against Victoria, England's twelfth man Warren Hegg kept wicket for the entire second innings of the match, achieving three dismissals. His appearance came about as a replacement for an injured Graham Thorpe, who withdrew from the match and the tour, flying back to London.

525 After taking 5 for 88 in the second innings of the second Test at Perth, Jason Gillespie was twelfth man for the third Test on his home ground, the Adelaide Oval. Chasing 443 for an improbable victory, England slipped from 5 for 221 to 237 all out, losing its last five wickets for 16 runs and the match by 205.

526 When an Australian XI took on the tourists in a four-day match at Hobart, each of the four innings featured an unbeaten century by one of the opening batsmen. England's Mike Atherton scored a maiden first-class double-century, finishing on 210*, while fellow opener Mark Butcher made an undefeated 103 in the second innings. The star of the match, though, was Greg Blewett who became the first Australian and just the fifth batsman overall to score an unbeaten century (169*) and double-century (213*) in the same first-class match. New South Welshman Corey Richards also hit a not-out century – 138 in the second innings, making it five for the match. Five substitute fielders, including national selector Allan Border, were used by Australia in the first innings.

527 Dean Headley took career-best Test figures of 6 for 60 as Australia disintegrated to 126 all out chasing a paltry 175 to win the fourth Test at Melbourne. Wicket-keeper Ian Healy reached 350 Test catches, with his opposite number, the debutant Warren Hegg, claiming his first. Hegg got his chance with Alec Stewart moving up to open the batting, a move that paid off when the captain scored a maiden Ashes century (107) and a further half-century (52), while his opening partner Mike Atherton made a pair.

528 Steve Waugh (96) fell four runs short of matching his brother Mark (121) who reached a century in the final Test at the SCG. Steve's dismissal saw him break West Indian Alvin Kallicharran's record of eight Test-match nineties. Darren Gough took 3 for 61, his three wickets forming the first hat-trick at Sydney since 1891-92. Michael Slater struck a hundred that came close to erasing one of the game's longest-surviving records. After escaping a run-out appeal on 35, Slater went on to 123 in the Australian second-innings total of 184, almost beating a record established by Charles Bannerman in the first-ever Test match, in Melbourne in 1876-77. Bannerman had celebrated the birth of Test cricket by scoring 165 – 67.35 per cent of Australia's total of 245 against England. Slater's 123 represented 66.85 per cent of the Australian scoreline, second only to Bannerman. Mark Taylor's catch of Mark Ramprakash in the second innings was his 157th in Tests, passing Allan Border's world record for most catches by a fielder, other than a wicket-keeper. S.C.G. MacGill took 12 wickets on the SCG pitch, including a match-winning haul of 7 for 50 as England fell for 188 chasing 287 for victory.

529 Michael Slater scored three second-innings centuries in the series, 113 in the first Test at Brisbane, 103 in the third at Adelaide and 123 in the fifth at Sydney. His three hundreds were the most by any batsman on either side; Steve Waugh the next best with two.

530 Australia was presented with a new crystal replica of the Ashes urn after winning the series 3-1.

531 Alan Mullally, who played Sheffield Shield cricket for Western Australia and Victoria, cut through the top order of Australia's star-studded line-up in the opening one-day international at Brisbane, accounting for the first four batsmen. He finished with his best-ever figures in one-day internationals, 4 for 18, and was named Man-of-the-Match.

532 Australia celebrated its national day on January 26 with a 16-run victory at the Adelaide Oval after a second consecutive ODI century in the series from Graeme Hick. The Zimbabwean-born Hick followed up an innings of 108 at Sydney with 109 at Adelaide and was named Man-of-the-Match, despite being on the losing side.

533 Under the captaincy of Shane Warne, Australia inflicted upon England one of its heaviest defeats in one-day internationals. England lost the second final in Melbourne, and its final match of the tour, by 162 runs, with Graeme Hick, Nasser Hussain and Neil Fairbrother all recording nought and Warne taking 3 for 16.

THE TOURISTS

A.J. Stewart (c), M.A. Atherton, M.A. Butcher, D.G. Cork,
J.P. Crawley, R.D.B. Croft, A.R.C. Fraser, D. Gough,
D.W. Headley, W.K. Hegg, B.C. Hollioake, N. Hussain,
A.D. Mullally, M.R. Ramprakash, P.M. Such, G.P. Thorpe,
A.J. Tudor. (Reinforcements & others who appeared in one-day internationals: M.W. Alleyne, M.A. Ealham,
N.H. Fairbrother, A.F. Giles, G.M. Hamilton, G.A. Hick,
A.J. Hollioake, N.V. Knight, I.D.K. Salisbury. V.J. Wells).

AUSTRALIA VERSUS ENGLAND 1861-2005

THE RESULTS

TEST MATCHES	FIRST-CLASS MATCHES	ALL MATCHES
P W L D	P W L D	P W L D
5 1 3 1	10 2 4 4	28 13 11 4

1st Test Brisbane: Drawn
2nd Test Perth: Australia won by 7 wickets
3rd Test Adelaide: Australia won by 205 runs
4th Test Melbourne: England won by 12 runs
5th Test Sydney: Australia won by 96 runs

2001
Tour of England

534 The Australians made 350-plus in both innings of its opening tour match against Worcestershire, with Damien Martyn (108) scoring a century on the first day. The hosts were bowled out twice for totals under 200, with captain Graeme Hick incurring a first-ball duck in the second innings.

535 West Australian team-mates dominated a tied limited-overs match at Northampton, with Damien Martyn top-scoring for the Australians and Mike Hussey for the hosts. Opening the batting with Adam Gilchrist, Martyn hit 101*, while Hussey, opening for Northamptonshire, made 73.

536 Chasing a modest 212 for victory in a one-day international at Manchester, England was bowled out for a record-low total of 86. A series of rain interruptions saw the Australian innings closed at 7 for 208 after 48 overs, and under the Duckworth-Lewis method England's target was calculated at 212, to be scored in 44 overs. Under heavy skies with a packed slips and gully cordon, England meekly surrendered in 32.4 overs and lost the match by 125 runs. Eighty-six was its lowest total in a one-day international since Australia had them out for 93 at Leeds in 1975.

537 Queensland bowler Joe Dawes took four Australian wickets before lunch on the opening day of the match against the MCC at Arundel. Dawes accounted for Justin Langer in each innings for scores of four and a duck, while Simon Katich enhanced his Test prospects with an unbeaten 168, off 167 balls, against an attack that also included the Pakistan pair of Azhar Mahmood and Shahid Afridi. Katich, in only his second match for an Australian XI, scored a century between lunch and tea, while New Zealand's Mark Richardson carried his bat for 64 in the MCC's first-innings total of 124.

538 In the lead-up to the opening Test, the Australians used the tour match against Essex at Chelmsford as batting practice, topping the 400-mark in both innings. The tourists began with a first-innings total of 5 declared for 405, highlighted by an unbeaten 251-run stand between Damien Martyn (114*) and Adam Gilchrist (150*). Gilchrist, the stand-in captain, reached his 150 off 149 balls, smacking 21 fours and three sixes in the process. After disposing of the home-side for 231, the Australians then surged to a monstrous 9 declared for 569, with half-centuries to Matthew Hayden (98), Michael Slater (58), Brett Lee (79), Ricky Ponting (79) and Colin Miller (62). At the time, the total was the fourth-highest in first-class history not to contain an individual century. Nine of the Essex XI had a go at trying to bowl out the visitors, including opening batsmen Nasser Hussain and Paul Grayson, and the wicket-keeper James Foster. Gilchrist declared 10 minutes before the scheduled close on the final day with a lead of 743: "I am sorry for the spectators. But it is not 100 per cent of the time we can keep everybody happy. Sometimes you have to be a little bit greedy. It is one of the very few times that the Australian cricket team has not gone out and had the paying public in mind all the time."

539 Both sides posted a 50-run partnership for the last wicket involving the wicket-keeper in the first innings of the first Test at Birmingham. England got proceedings underway with a total of 294, punctuated by a 10th-wicket stand of 103 between Alec Stewart (65) and Andy Caddick (49*), the No.11 hitting seven fours and a six in his 40-ball romp. Australia responded with an imposing, and ultimately match-winning, total of 576 that included centuries from numbers five through seven and a half-century stand for the last wicket between wicket-keeper Adam Gilchrist and Glenn McGrath. Steve Waugh made 105, as did Damien Martyn, while Gilchrist chipped in with 152 and put on 63 for the 10th wicket, in which McGrath made just one, the first time that a 50-run stand in a Test match had seen the No.11 contribute so few runs. Gilchrist's 152, scored on his Ashes debut, overtook Alan Knott's 135 at Nottingham in 1977 as the highest innings by a wicket-keeper in an Anglo-Australian

Test. One of Mark Butcher's overs sent down to Gilchrist cost 22 runs, equalling the most expensive over in Ashes history. England went down by an innings and 118 runs, losing their last seven wickets for 22 runs in the second innings. Bowled out for just 164, only Marcus Trescothick displayed any defiance, hitting 76 after suffering a first-innings duck.

540 Ricky Ponting marked his first match as captain with a century and a win when the Australians took on Somerset in a four-day match at Taunton. The home-side fielded two guest players, with Pakistan fast bowler Shoaib Akhtar bringing Ponting's innings to a close at 128, while Aamer Sohail (50) was the only batsman to reach fifty in Somerset's first innings. The Australians won the match by 176 runs, after 176* from Damien Martyn.

541 Glenn McGrath took 5 for 54 in England's first innings in the second Test at Lord's, while his partner Jason Gillespie claimed the almost-identical figures of 5 for 53 in the second. Mark Waugh scored the only century (108) of the match, and then set a new world record for catches when England's No.11 Darren Gough became his 158th victim in the second innings.

542 The Australians went into the tour match against Hampshire at Southampton with only four specialist batsmen, a move that contributed to the tourists' first loss to the county since 1912. The Australians were routed for 97 in the first innings, with Alan Mullally taking 5 for 18 and debutant James Schofield 3 for 25, dismissing Matthew Hayden for one with his first ball in first-class cricket. He then accounted for Justin Langer for two in his third over and later picked up the prized scalp of Steve Waugh for 10.

543 England's captain Mike Atherton fell for a duck to the second ball of the third Test at Nottingham. It was his 20th duck, an England record, relieving Derek Underwood of the unwanted milestone. After accounting for Atherton, Glenn McGrath went on to take another four wickets, finishing with 5 for 49, while a recalled Alex Tudor claimed 5 for 44 in Australia's first innings. Jason Gillespie reached the milestone of 100 Test wickets, while Shane Warne claimed his 100th Ashes wicket. Australia regained the Ashes with a seven-wicket victory, its seventh series win over England on the trot.

544 Despite a 202-run first-wicket partnership between Murray Goodwin (105) and Richard Montgomerie (157) – the only double-century opening stand against the Australians on tour – Sussex went down by eight wickets after second-innings hundreds from Adam

Gilchrist (114) and Ricky Ponting (147*). Gilchrist, promoted to open the innings, hit 19 fours and two sixes in his 102-ball stay.

545 With Steve Waugh sidelined because of a calf injury, stand-in captain Adam Gilchrist presided over the Leeds Test in which England reached a victory target of 315, after the wicket-keeper had declared Australia's second innings on the fourth afternoon. Marking the 300th Anglo-Australian Test, Gilchrist became the first Australian captain to lose a Test after making a declaration. Mark Butcher was England's hero, smashing an unbeaten 173 with 24 boundaries. In England's first innings, Glenn McGrath reached the milestone of 350 Test wickets, while Alec Stewart (76*) batted as low as No.7 for the first time in his 114 Tests to date.

546 On consecutive Ashes tours Glenn McGrath claimed identical first-innings hauls of 7 for 76 in a Test match, yet ended up on the losing side both times. The first came in 1997 when Australia was dismissed for 104 in the sixth Test at The Oval chasing a victory-target of just 124, the third occasion during that year they had lost the final match of a series they had already won. In 2001, and again with the Ashes theirs, Australia surrendered the fourth Test at Leeds where McGrath was the pick of the bowlers, taking eight wickets in the match.

547 Australia bounced back after its loss at Leeds with a match-winning 4 declared for 641 at The Oval, a total that included half-centuries from the top five in the batting order – Matthew Hayden 68, Justin Langer 102 retired hurt, Ricky Ponting 62, Mark Waugh 120 and Steve Waugh, who hit an unbeaten 157. In their final Ashes appearance together, the Waughs matched the efforts of Ian and Greg Chappell, who back in 1972 both scored centuries in the same innings in Australia's win at The Oval. Mike Atherton's final Test match saw him dismissed for a record 19th time by Glenn McGrath.

548 The average age of the touring party under Steve Waugh was 30, Australia's oldest since Don Bradman's 1948 'Invincibles'. Australia secured the Ashes in just 11 match days' play. In his four Tests on tour Waugh topped the averages with 321 runs at 107.00.

THE TOURISTS

S.R. Waugh (c), M.G. Bevan, N.W. Bracken, D.W. Fleming,
A.C. Gilchrist, J.N. Gillespie, I.J. Harvey, M.L. Hayden,
S.M. Katich, J.L. Langer, B. Lee, G.D. McGrath,
D.R. Martyn, C.R. Miller, R.T. Ponting, M.J. Slater,

A. Symonds, S.K. Warne, M.E. Waugh.
(Reinforcements: A.A. Noffke, W.A. Seccombe).

THE RESULTS

TEST MATCHES	FIRST-CLASS MATCHES	ALL MATCHES
P W L D	P W L D	P W L D T NR
5 4 1 0	11 8 2 1	21 13 4 1 1 2

1st Test Birmingham: Australia won by an innings and 118 runs
2nd Test Lord's: Australia won by 8 wickets
3rd Test Nottingham: Australia won by 7 wickets
4th Test Leeds: England won by 6 wickets
5th Test The Oval: Australia won by an innings and 25 runs

2002-03
TOUR OF AUSTRALIA

549 Even before the tour began England's party suffered the loss of star batsman Graham Thorpe, burdened following the break-up of his marriage. Darren Gough, overcoming a knee operation, and Andrew Flintoff, a hernia operation, both made the trip, but neither played in a Test. England used as many as 30 players in first-class and limited-overs matches during the summer.

550 England began its tour with a loss in the Lilac Hill festival match to the ACB Chairman's XI that featured a 47-year-old David Hookes and a 49-year-old Wayne Clark. Western Australia's Kade Harvey hit an entertaining 114 off 88 balls in his team's 7 for 301, while Simon Jones conceded 43 runs from his final three overs.

551 Martin Love scored Queensland's fifth-highest first-class innings with a nine-hour 250 against the tourists at the Allan Border Field. He was the backbone of three consecutive century partnerships, 128 for the third wicket with Stuart Law (68), 105 with Andrew Symonds (47) and 125 with Lee Carseldine (51).

552 Nasser Hussain won the toss and sent Australia in to bat in the first Test at Brisbane, a decision that backfired big-time. England's fastest bowler Simon Jones was stretchered off the ground, not to be seen for the rest of the summer after injuring his right knee while fielding. Australia made 492 in its first innings, despite four batsmen in the line-up failing to get off the mark. Glenn McGrath reached the milestone of 100 Ashes wickets, while Matthew Hayden joined the ranks of some of Ashes' immortals, Herbert Sutcliffe, Walter Hammond and Denis Compton included, by scoring a century in each innings – 197 and 103 – for a match total of exactly 300 runs. Australia shot out England for 79 to secure its biggest Ashes win by a runs margin (384) on home soil. A rare incident took place earlier in proceedings when Craig White, who had been called up earlier in the tour from Adelaide club cricket, bowled to his brother-in-law Darren Lehmann.

553 Martin Love scored his second double-century of the summer against the tourists within a fortnight, reaching 201* while representing an Australian XI (3d-353) in a three-day match at Hobart. Love came to the crease when the opening ball of the match forced Matthew Elliott to retire after he was hit on the elbow, courtesy of Alex Tudor. Love passed the milestone of 10,000 first-class runs, while England was forced to follow-on after Brad Williams had taken 5 for 52 in an all-out first-innings total of just 183. Robert Key averted disaster for the England XI in the second innings by scoring an unbeaten 174.

554 England opener Michael Vaughan starred with the bat, scoring 177 and 41 in the second Test at Adelaide, but England went down by an innings and 51 runs. Matthew Hoggard finished the match with 1 for 84, having returned figures of 0 for 122 and 0 for 42 in the first Test at Brisbane.

555 Australia cleaned up a down-and-out England with another innings victory in Perth, taking a 3-0 lead and capturing the Ashes for the eighth time in a row. Mark Butcher was fined $2000 for hitting the stumps with his bat after making a duck in the second innings, while Alex Tudor needed six stitches after being decked by a Brett Lee bouncer.

556 As a lead-up to the VB Series one-day internationals, the tourists lost three limited-overs match in a row. New South Wales claimed victory by eight wickets in a day-night affair at the SCG, Australia A beat them by 23 runs two days later at the same venue, and they then suffered a four-wicket loss at the hands of the Prime Minister's XI at Canberra's Manuka Oval.

557 Despite reaching a highly respectable 8 for 251 in the first match of the VB Series in Sydney, England ended up losing once again. Nick Knight remained unbeaten at the end of England's 50 overs with 111, sharing in a first-wicket stand of 101 with Marcus Trescothick (60). Australia responded with an identical opening partnership between Adam Gilchrist (53) and Matthew Hayden (98), cruising to victory with five overs to spare and seven wickets in hand. Two days later England finally tasted success, winning its first match on tour after two months with a 43-run ODI victory over Sri Lanka at Brisbane.

558 Justin Langer became the second batsman of the summer to post an innings of 250 against England, while his opening partner Matthew Hayden scored 102 in the first innings of the fourth Test in Melbourne. Their stand of 195 obliterated the long-standing Ashes MCG record of 126 between Victor Trumper (63) and Monty Noble (64) from the 1907-08 series. Martin Love, who had earlier scored 250 in the state match in Brisbane, was granted his Test debut and responded with an unbeaten 62.

559 For the first time in 12 years, Australia went into a Test match against England without the services of their star duo Glenn McGrath and Shane Warne. England's first-day effort in the final Test at Sydney was punctuated by a 166-run third-wicket stand between Mark Butcher (124) and Nasser Hussain (75), breaking Walter Hammond and Maurice Leyland's SCG record of 129 established in 1936-37. Remarkably, the record was broken again within three days when Michael Vaughan (183) and Hussain (72) kept each other company while 189 runs were added for the same wicket in the second innings. Steve Waugh equalled Allan Border's world record of 156 Test match appearances, and batting against hints that his time was up as a Test cricketer hit a pulsating century that was brought up off the final ball of the second day's play. En route to his 29th Test ton (102), Waugh became only the third batsman after Border and India's Sunil Gavaskar to reach the milestone of 10,000 Test runs. England went on to gain its first victory at the SCG since 1978-79 and only first-class win of the tour. Andy Caddick took 10 wickets (3-121 & 7-94) in what turned out to be his final Test appearance.

560 Although making a duck in the first innings of the SCG Test, Michael Vaughan was named Man-of-the-Match after scoring 183 in the second. The opening batsman was a lone success story for the tourists, also snaring the Man-of-the-Series award for his 633 runs and three centuries.

THE TOURISTS

N. Hussain (c), M.A. Butcher, A.R. Caddick, J.P. Crawley,
R.K.J. Dawson, A. Flintoff, J.S. Foster, A.F. Giles, D. Gough,
S.J. Harmison, M.J. Hoggard, S.P. Jones, R.W.T. Key,
A.J. Stewart, M.E. Trescothick, M.P. Vaughan.
(Reinforcements & others who appeared in one-day
internationals: J.M. Anderson, G.J. Batty, I.D. Blackwell,
P.D. Collingwood, A.J. Hollioake, R.C. Irani, R.J. Kirtley,
N.V. Knight, C.M.W. Read, O.A. Shah, C.E.W. Silverwood,
J.N. Snape, A.J. Tudor, C. White).

THE RESULTS

TEST MATCHES				FIRST-CLASS MATCHES				ALL MATCHES			
P	W	L	D	P	W	L	D	P	W	L	D
5	1	4	0	8	1	4	3	22	4	14	4

1st Test Brisbane: Australia won by 384 runs
2nd Test Adelaide: Australia won by an innings and 51 runs
3rd Test Perth: Australia won by an innings and 48 runs
4th Test Melbourne: Australia won by 5 wickets
5th Test Sydney: England won by 225 runs

2005
TOUR OF ENGLAND

561 The inaugural Anglo-Australian Twenty20 match, played at the Rose Bowl in Southampton, saw the home side win the event by a margin of exactly 100 runs. England, in its debut Twenty20 match, smacked a total of 179 runs off 20 overs and then disposed of Australia for just 79. Andrew Symonds, Michael Clarke and Ricky Ponting all made ducks.

562 The Australians travelled to Taunton and faced a Somerset XI, whose innings was opened by the international double of

South Africa's Graeme Smith and Sri Lanka's Sanath Jayasuriya. After the Australians piled on a massive 342 off its 50 overs, Somerset got things off to a flier with a match-winning first-wicket partnership of 197, Smith hitting 108 and Jayasuriya 101. Smith made his 100 in 85 minutes off 68 balls with 17 boundaries, while his partner reached triple figures off 77 balls with nine fours and three sixes. Brett Lee left the field after conceding 26 runs off fours overs, while Michael Kasprowicz was belted for 89 off eight.

563 After copping a humiliating five-wicket defeat at the hands of Bangladesh at Sophia Gardens, Australia then suffered another one-day international loss the following day at Bristol. England took the honours after a 65-ball unbeaten 91 from Kevin Pietersen, and 5 for 33 by Steve Harmison, who accounted for Ricky Ponting (0) and Damien Martyn (0) in the space of three deliveries. England's openers, Marcus Trescothick and Andrew Strauss, fell in identical fashion, both bowled for 16 by Glenn McGrath.

564 In the NatWest Series match at Chester-le-Street, Darren Gough (46*) and No.11 Steve Harmison (11*) put on 50 runs in partnership, establishing England's first-ever half-century last-wicket stand in a one-day international. Gough top-scored for England in its total of 9 for 209 and beat Angus Fraser's 38* against Australia at Melbourne in 1990-91 as England's highest ODI score by a No.10 batsman.

565 Geraint Jones became the first England wicket-keeper to achieve five dismissals in a one-day international against Australia, doing so in the match at Edgbaston. Darren Gough set another record, becoming the first England bowler to concede 70 runs in a ODI innings at Edgbaston, returning figures of 9-0-70-3.

566 During the tied NatWest Series final at Lord's, England sent down 28 consecutive deliveries without conceding a run. A rather subdued Andrew Symonds faced 16 of the balls, and Michael Clarke 12, in one of the driest spells ever witnessed in a one-day international. Symonds made 29 off 71 balls, and Clarke two off 19. Geraint Jones became the first England keeper to score a half-century (71) and achieve five dismissals in a one-day international against Australia, and only the third overall. Australia's 196 was its lowest total in a 50-overs one-day international at Lord's.

567 In the opening match of the second one-day international series of the tour, played at Leeds, England recorded century partnerships for the first two wickets of a ODI against Australia for the first time. Marcus Trescothick shared an opening partnership of 101 with Andrew Strauss (41) and then an unbroken stand of 120 with Michael Vaughan (59*). Trescothick scored his maiden ODI hundred (104*) against Australia, guiding England to its first-ever nine-wicket victory over Australia in a one-day international.

568 Brett Lee became the first Australian bowler to capture five wickets in a one-day international against England at Lord's, snaring 5 for 41. Ricky Ponting's 111 made him only the third Australian to score a one-day international century against England at the home of cricket, after Graeme Wood (114*) in 1985 and Geoff Marsh (111*) in 1989.

569 Australia's final one-day international of the summer, at The Oval, was its 600th overall. Brett Lee celebrated the occasion by reaching the milestone of 200 wickets in his 112th match, the quickest by a fast bowler, beating South African Allan Donald's mark of 117. Opening the batting, Adam Gilchrist (121*) became the first wicket-keeper to score a one-day international century against England in England. Glenn McGrath finished the three-match campaign with one wicket for 103, his worst-ever return in a ODI series.

570 The Australians' final first-class hit-out before the opening Test saw Stuart MacGill claim six wickets in the match against Leicestershire, including that of West Australian import Chris Rogers who clouted a memorable match-saving maiden double-century. Opening the innings with Darren Robinson (81), the Sydney-born Rogers made 209 in a first-wicket stand of 247, after their first-innings partnership of nought.

571 Not since 1890 had both Australia (190) and England (155) failed to muster 200 in the first innings of a Test match at Lord's. Kevin Pietersen (57 & 64*) became the eighth England batsman to score two half-centuries on his Test debut, while Matthew Hoggard bagged the second pair of his Test career, after suffering two ducks at Sydney in 2002-03. England finished the match with its last eight batsmen dismissed in the second innings failing to reach double figures.

572 In his three Test appearances at Lord's, Glenn McGrath took five wickets in the first innings of each match. He marked the 2005 Test by reaching the coveted milestone of 500 wickets, doing so in record-fast time (110 Tests) for a fast bowler. McGrath took 5 for 53 in England's first-innings total of 155, accounting for the first five in the batting order, none of whom reached double figures – Marcus Trescothick with four, Andrew Strauss two, Michael Vaughan three, Ian Bell six and Andrew Flintoff nought. McGrath's opposite number Steve Harmison was also in fine form, applying punishing blows on the arm of Justin Langer and to the helmets of Matthew Hayden and Ricky Ponting, who later required plastic surgery for injuries to a cut cheek. Entrusted with the opening over of a Test for the first time in his career, Harmison finished the first day of the series with 5 for 43; McGrath with 5 for 21.

573 Glenn McGrath was uniquely named Man-of-the-Match in each of his three Test appearances at Lord's, after returning match-figures of 9 for 103 (8-38 & 1-65) in 1997, 8 for 114 (5-54 & 3-60) in 2001 and 9 for 82 (5-53 & 4-29) in 2005.

574 In the second Test against at Edgbaston, Marcus Trescothick (90) and Andrew Strauss (48) posted England's first century opening partnership (112) in 36 innings against Australia. The previous occasion had been at Nottingham in 1997, when Mike Atherton (27) and Alec Stewart (87) added 106 for the first wicket. After being put in to bat by Ricky Ponting England made 407 on the back of the 112-run stand, the highest score in a day's play at the ground, and its fifth-best against Australia overall. Brett Lee had opening-day figures of 17-1-111-1, returning an economy rate of over 100 (per 100 balls of 10 overs or more) for the third time in an innings in his career, a new Test record.

575 The Edgbaston Test saw Shane Warne become the first bowler to achieve the milestone of 100 Test wickets in a country other than his own. It came with a delivery in the second innings – eerily reminiscent of the now-famous Mike Gatting dismissal in 1993 – that ripped through the defences of Andrew Strauss crashing onto his middle stump. Warne achieved the unique feat in his 19th Test in England, the previous record-holder being Dennis Lillee who took 96 wickets in 16 Tests in England. Warne claimed another two firsts – with his figures of 10 for 162 he became the first Australian to take 10 wickets in a Test at Edgbaston, and he was the first Australian to be dismissed 'hit wicket' at the ground. Brett Lee (43*) and Michael Kasprowicz (20) put on a plucky 59 for the last wicket, brought to an end three runs shy of victory when the Queenslander nicked one through to the wicket-keeeper. England's nail-biting two-run win is the second-narrowest victory margin in Test history, after the West Indies beat Australia by one run at Adelaide in 1992-93.

576 For the first time since 1981, no batsman scored a century in the first two Tests of an Ashes series. Michael Clarke, with 91, came the closest to triple figures in the opening Test, while the second Test, with a healthy 1176 runs scored, was also devoid of an individual hundred. Six half-centuries were scored, the highest being 90 by Marcus Trescothick.

577 Shane Warne became the first bowler to capture 600 wickets when he dismissed Marcus Trescothick on the first morning of the third Test at Manchester. The opening combination of Justin Langer and Matthew Hayden posted a maiden half-century stand (58) against England, after previous efforts of 8, 36, 5, 35, 18, 0 and 47. Adam Gilchrist made 30 in the first innings, becoming the highest-scoring Test-match wicket-keeper of all time, while Glenn McGrath marked his 111th Test by becoming the highest-scoring No.11 batsman in the game's history. At the end of the match McGrath had taken his tally of runs scored at No.11 to 556, overtaking the previous record of 553 by the West Indies' Courtney Walsh.

578 South Australia's Shaun Tait warmed up for his Test debut with some brutal fast bowling in the match against Northamptonshire, hitting Tim Roberts on the head and drawing blood. It forced the opener's retirement from the match in which his team-mate Ben Phillips was also forced to retire, albeit temporarily, after being struck on the head by a ball from Glenn McGrath.

579 After England made 477 in the fourth Test at Nottingham, Australia (218) was forced to follow-on for the first time in 17 years since playing Pakistan at Karachi in 1988-89. In his fourth appearance at Trent Bridge, Shane Warne (4-102) reached 25 wickets in Test matches at the venue, the first visiting bowler to achieve the milestone, overtaking Richard Hadlee's 24 wickets in five Tests. When he nabbed Ashley Giles leg-before in the first innings, Warne beat Wasim Akram's record of 119 lbw dismissals in Test-match cricket.

580 Substitute fielder Gray Pratt ran out Ricky Ponting in the Nottingham Test, with the Australian captain fined for venting his spleen at the England dressing-room. The dismissal, though, earned one of Pratt's old school friends a £3400 ($6000) windfall after he'd placed a bet in 2003 that the Durham player would represent England within five years. Bookmakers William Hill paid out on the bet even though Pratt didn't officially play for England.

581 The final day of the fourth Test attracted a record television audience in Britain, with figures reaching 8.4 million. The previous record was 7.7 million during the third Test, and for the final of *Big Brother*.

582 A two-day county match prior to the final Test was a high-scoring affair with 1000 runs creamed off the bat from exactly 200 overs. Essex became the first team to extract 500 runs off an Australian

XI on the first day of a match, making 4 declared for 502 off 105 overs, with Alistair Cook scoring 214 and Ravinder Bopara 135. The Australians responded with 6 for 561 off 95 overs, with Matthew Hayden contributing 150 and Brad Hodge 166. The two days witnessed a total of 145 fours and 18 sixes. Although the match did not attract first-class status, the fixture revived memories of the 1948 match between the two sides when the Australians amassed a world-record first-class score of 721 on the opening day.

583 The final Test at The Oval, a draw that gave England the prize it had sought for so long, was another personal triumph for Shane Warne. He took 6 for 122 in the first innings and 6 for 124 in the second, his best-ever return (12-246) in a Test match against England. He became the first bowler to claim 10 wickets in consecutive Tests at The Oval, and the fourth to claim 10 Test victims on four occasions against England. Warne's county team-mate Kevin Pietersen ended the summer with a bang, blasting seven sixes during his maiden Test century of 158, a record number in an Ashes innings, beating Ian Botham's six at Manchester in 1981. Pietersen completed the series as the highest run-scorer on either side with 473 at 52.55. After innings of 12, 34, 0, 31, 34, 36, 7 and 26 Matthew Hayden scored his first fifty of the series, proceeding to 105 and adding 185 for the first wicket with Justin Langer, who also scored a century (138). Hayden and Langer became the first visiting pair to establish two century-opening stands at The Oval, after making 158 in 2001.

584 Shane Warne took 40 wickets in the five Tests of the summer, average 19.92, the third-best haul by a spinner in a Test series, after England's Jim Laker (46 v Australia 1956) and Australia's Clarrie Grimmett (44 v South Africa 1935-36). He also became only the third bowler to take 40 wickets and end up on the losing side, after Terry Alderman (42) in England in 1981 and Rodney Hogg (41) against England in Australia in 1978-79. Warne took the wickets of Andrew Strauss and Ashley Giles six times each, and with the bat hit 249 runs at an average of 27.66, finishing ahead of the likes of Simon Katich (248 runs at 27.55), Adam Gilchrist (181 at 26.62) and Damien Martyn (178 at 19.77).

585 All the glory gained by Shane Warne on the field came against a backdrop of off-field shenanigans. The British tabloids were relentless throughout the campaign, making Warne's private life front-page news from day one.

586 The two Test matches that England won were both notable for the absence of Glenn McGrath. After his Man-of-the-Match performance in the first Test at Lord's, where he took nine wickets (5-53 & 4-29), McGrath was unavailable for the second after stepping on a ball during a pre-match warm-up and hurting his ankle. England went on to win by two runs: "I was just standing there with Brad Haddin. I turned to chase a ball, and my first step planted straight on top of a cricket ball that was on the ground. I'd seen them laid out earlier and thought how neat they looked. It was just one of those things. I knew before I hit the ground that I was out of the match." McGrath was also ruled out of the fourth Test at Trent Bridge, with England claiming victory by three wickets.

587 England used just 12 players in the entire series, the only change forced through an injury suffered by Simon Jones who topped their averages with 18 wickets at 21.00. England was on course to use the same XI for the first time since 1884-85, when William Scotton, Arthur Shrewsbury, George Ulyett, Billy Barnes, Willie Bates, Wilfred Flowers, Maurice Read, Johnny Briggs, William Attewell, Bobby Peel and Joe Hunter played in the five-Test series against Australia. England had used 17 players in the 2002-03 series, 19 in 2001, 17 in 1998-99 and 18 in 1997.

588 By the end of the third Test England had blasted a record 26 sixes, finishing the five-match series with 36. The previous highest number of sixes in a Test series against Australia was 23 by South Africa in five Tests in 1966-67. The total of 51 sixes struck by England and Australia established a new high for any series in Test-match cricket.

589 For the first time since the 1978-79 series, Australia failed to reach 400 in an innings. The tourists' highest total was 387 in the fourth Test at Nottingham, and 384 in the first Test at Lord's.

590 Andrew Flintoff was England's undoubted star of the summer, becoming the first all-rounder from his country to achieve the double of 400 runs and 20 wickets in a Test series against Australia. With the bat he scored 402 runs, average 40.20, and with the ball claimed 24 wickets at 27.29. He was named 'Player of the Year' by the Professional Cricketers' Association and also won the BBC's 'Sports Personality of the Year' award.

591 Jason Gillespie finished at the bottom of the heap in the series' bowling averages for both teams, dropped at the end of the third Test after taking just three wickets for 300, average 100.00. Ricky Ponting topped the Test and first-class bowling averages with one wicket at 9.00.

592 In celebration of England regaining the Ashes, an estimated 25,000 people flocked to Trafalgar Square to salute the England players who were transported through the streets of London on an open-top, double-decker bus. The players then attended a function hosted by the Prime Minister Tony Blair at No.10 Downing Street.

593 Prior to the Ashes getting underway, England's cricket hierarchy wanted its team to have three so-called 'superstars' who could be recognised by 10 per cent of the population within six years. After the Ashes were won, it appeared their vision had been realised within six months. A street survey of 100 people in London by a leading cricket magazine found that 75 per cent recognised Andrew Flintoff, 18 per cent were able to identify the entire team, with 25 per cent of women under the age of 26 identifying more than half the players.

594 After becoming the first England captain in two decades to regain the Ashes, Michael Vaughan was granted the freedom of the city of Sheffield. He became just the sixth honorary freeman of the Yorkshire city, joining the illustrious company of Winston Churchill and Nelson Mandela. Other members of the team were afforded a similar honour, including Andrew Flintoff in the city of Preston and Marcus Trescothick in Keynsham.

595 Britain's national postal service, Royal Mail, commemorated England's Ashes success with a set of stamps. It signalled the first occasion that living people other than members of the Royal Family had appeared on a UK stamp.

596 A song that became England's unofficial theme throughout the campaign was later recorded by the players and classical singer Keedie. 'Jerusalem' was released as a CD single and made its way into the UK Top 20, with proceeds going to help those devastated by a powerful earthquake that struck southern Asia in October 2005.

597 In a vote conducted by the Cricinfo website to select the best composite Ashes XI after the five Tests, Shane Warne received the most votes, with 4526. The team comprised six England players and five Australians: Justin Langer, Marcus Trescothick, Ricky Ponting, Michael Vaughan (c), Kevin Pietersen, Andrew Flintoff, Adam Gilchrist (wk), Shane Warne, Simon Jones, Steve Harmison and Glenn McGrath.

598 Australia reclaimed the services of England bowling coach Troy Cooley who was widely credited as being a key factor in it regaining the Ashes. Cooley, who appeared in 33 first-class matches for

Tasmania, accepted a coaching role with Cricket Australia not long after the Ashes went to England.

599 On the back of the Ashes victory, and after a five-year wait, England's Zimbabwean-born coach Duncan Fletcher was granted UK citizenship. His request for citizenship had always been rejected by authorities, citing that he spent too many days away from Britain – touring with the England team – to be eligible.

600 The entire England team and its coach featured in The Queen's 2006 New Year Honours List, with Michael Vaughan named an Officer of the Order of the British Empire. The rest of the squad received an MBE.

THE TOURISTS

R.T. Ponting (c), M.J. Clarke, A.C. Gilchrist, J.N. Gillespie,
B.J. Haddin, M.L. Hayden, B.J. Hodge, M.S. Kasprowicz,
S.M. Katich, J.L. Langer, B. Lee, S.C.G. MacGill,
G.D. McGrath, D.R. Martyn, S.W. Tait, S.K. Warne.
Others who appeared in one-day internationals: G.B. Hogg,
M.E.K. Hussey, A. Symonds, S.R. Watson.
(Reinforcement: S.R. Clark).

THE RESULTS

TEST MATCHES	FIRST-CLASS MATCHES	ALL MATCHES
P W L D	P W L D	P W L D T NR
5 1 2 2	7 1 2 4	24 8 7 6 1 2

1st Test Lord's: Australia won by 239 runs
2nd Test Birmingham: England won by 2 runs
3rd Test Manchester: Drawn
4th Test Nottingham: England won by 3 wickets
5th Test The Oval: Drawn

AUSTRALIA VERSUS ENGLAND TEST MATCH RESULTS
1877-2005

CAPTAINS

SEASON	AUSTRALIA	ENGLAND	T	A	E	D	ASHES
1876-77	Dave Gregory	James Lillywhite	2	1	1	0	-
1878-79	Dave Gregory	Lord Harris	1	1	0	0	-
1880	Billy Murdoch	Lord Harris	1	0	1	0	-
1881-82	Billy Murdoch	Alfred Shaw	4	2	0	2	-
1882	Billy Murdoch	A.N. 'Monkey' Hornby	1	1	0	0	-
1882-83	Billy Murdoch	Hon. Ivo Bligh	4	2	2	0	E
1884	Billy Murdoch	Lord Harris (1)	3	0	1	2	E
1884-85	Tim Horan (2)	Arthur Shrewsbury	5	2	3	0	E
1886	'Tup' Scott	Allan Steel	3	0	3	0	E
1886-87	Percy McDonnell	Arthur Shrewsbury	2	0	2	0	E
1887-88	Percy McDonnell	Walter Read	1	0	1	0	E
1888	Percy McDonnell	W.G. Grace (3)	3	1	2	0	E
1890	Billy Murdoch	W.G. Grace	2	0	2	0	E
1891-92	Jack Blackham	W.G. Grace	3	2	1	0	A
1893	Jack Blackham	W.G. Grace (4)	3	0	1	2	E
1894-95	George Giffen (5)	Andrew Stoddart	5	2	3	0	E
1896	'Harry' Trott	W.G. Grace	3	1	2	0	E
1897-98	'Harry' Trott	Andrew Stoddart (6)	5	4	1	0	A
1899	Joe Darling	Archie MacLaren (7)	5	1	0	4	A
1901-02	Joe Darling (8)	Archie MacLaren	5	4	1	0	A
1902	Joe Darling	Archie MacLaren	5	2	1	2	A
1903-04	Monty Noble	'Plum' Warner	5	2	3	0	E
1905	Joe Darling	F.S. Jackson	5	0	2	3	E
1907-08	Monty Noble	Arthur Jones (9)	5	4	1	0	A
1909	Monty Noble	Archie MacLaren	5	2	1	2	A
1911-12	Clem Hill	Johnny Douglas	5	1	4	0	E
1912	Syd Gregory	C.B. Fry	3	0	1	2	E
1920-21	Warwick Armstrong	Johnny Douglas	5	5	0	0	A
1921	Warwick Armstrong	Lionel Tennyson (10)	5	3	0	2	A
1924-25	Herbie Collins	Arthur Gilligan	5	4	1	0	A
1926	Herbie Collins (11)	Arthur Carr (12)	5	0	1	4	E
1928-29	Jack Ryder	Percy Chapman (13)	5	1	4	0	E
1930	Bill Woodfull	Percy Chapman (14)	5	2	1	2	A
1932-33	Bill Woodfull	Douglas Jardine	5	1	4	0	E
1934	Bill Woodfull	Bob Wyatt (15)	5	2	1	2	A
1936-37	Don Bradman	'Gubby' Allen	5	3	2	0	A
1938	Don Bradman	Walter Hammond	4	1	1	2	A
1946-47	Don Bradman	Walter Hammond (16)	5	3	0	2	A
1948	Don Bradman	Norman Yardley	5	4	0	1	A
1950-51	Lindsay Hassett	Freddie Brown	5	4	1	0	A

600 MEMORABLE MOMENTS

Year	Australia Captain	England Captain	T	A	E	D	Result
1953	Lindsay Hassett	Len Hutton	5	0	1	4	E
1954-55	Ian Johnson (17)	Len Hutton	5	1	3	1	E
1956	Ian Johnson	Peter May	5	1	2	2	E
1958-59	Richie Benaud	Peter May	5	4	0	1	A
1961	Richie Benaud (18)	Peter May (19)	5	2	1	2	A
1962-63	Richie Benaud	Ted Dexter	5	1	1	3	A
1964	Bob Simpson	Ted Dexter	5	1	0	4	A
1965-66	Bob Simpson (20)	Mike Smith	5	1	1	3	A
1968	Bill Lawry (21)	Colin Cowdrey (22)	5	1	1	3	A
1970-71	Bill Lawry (23)	Ray Illingworth	6	0	2	4	E
1972	Ian Chappell	Ray Illingworth	5	2	2	1	E
1974-75	Ian Chappell	Mike Denness (24)	6	4	1	1	A
1975	Ian Chappell	Tony Greig (25)	4	1	0	3	A
1976-77	Greg Chappell	Tony Greig	1	1	0	0	-
1977	Greg Chappell	Mike Brearley	5	0	3	2	E
1978-79	Graham Yallop	Mike Brearley	6	1	5	0	E
1979-80	Greg Chappell	Mike Brearley	3	3	0	0	-
1980	Greg Chappell	Ian Botham	1	0	0	1	-
1981	Kim Hughes	Mike Brearley (26)	6	1	3	2	E
1982-83	Greg Chappell	Bob Willis	5	2	1	2	A
1985	Allan Border	David Gower	6	1	3	2	E
1986-87	Allan Border	Mike Gatting	5	1	2	2	E
1987-88	Allan Border	Mike Gatting	1	0	0	1	-
1989	Allan Border	David Gower	6	4	0	2	A
1990-91	Allan Border	Graham Gooch (27)	5	3	0	2	A
1993	Allan Border	Graham Gooch (28)	6	4	1	1	A
1994-95	Mark Taylor	Mike Atherton	5	3	1	1	A
1997	Mark Taylor	Mike Atherton	6	3	2	1	A
1998-99	Mark Taylor	Alec Stewart	5	3	1	1	A
2001	Steve Waugh (29)	Nasser Hussain (30)	5	4	1	0	A
2002-03	Steve Waugh	Nasser Hussain	5	4	1	0	A
2005	Ricky Ponting	Michael Vaughan	5	1	2	2	E
	Tests in Australia		**160**	**80**	**54**	**26**	
	Tests in England		**151**	**46**	**43**	**62**	
	Totals		**311**	**126**	**97**	**88**	

(1) A.N. 'Monkey' Hornby captained the 1st Test (2) Billy Murdoch 1st, Hugh Massie 3rd, Jack Blackham 4th (3) Allan Steel 1st (4) Andrew Stoddart 1st (5) Jack Blackham 1st (6) Archie MacLaren 1st, 2nd, 5th (7) W.G. Grace 1st (8) Hugh Trumble 4th, 5th (9) Frederick Fane 1st, 2nd, 3rd (10) Johnny Douglas 1st, 2nd (11) Warren Bardsley 3rd, 4th (12) Percy Chapman 5th (13) Jack White 5th (14) Bob Wyatt 5th (15) Cyril Walters 1st (16) Norman Yardley 5th (17) Arthur Morris 2nd (18) Neil Harvey 2nd (19) Colin Cowdrey 1st, 2nd (20) Brian Booth 1st, 3rd (21) Barry Jarman 4th (22) Tom Graveney 4th (23) Ian Chappell 7th (24) John Edrich 4th (25) Mike Denness 1st (26) Ian Botham 1st, 2nd (27) Allan Lamb 1st (28) Mike Atherton 5th, 6th (29) Adam Gilchrist 4th (30) Mike Atherton 2nd, 3rd.